Kenneth Slessor

Selected Poems

Introduction by
Dennis Haskell
Notes by the Author

Angus&Robertson
An imprint of HarperCollins*Publishers*

Angus&Robertson
An imprint of HarperCollins*Publishers*, Australia

First published in Australia as *One Hundred Poems*
by Angus & Robertson Publishers in 1944
Published as *Poems* in 1957
First published as *Selected Poems* in 1975
First A&R Modern Poets edition 1977
Second A&R Modern Poets edition 1988
This edition 1993
by HarperCollins*Publishers* Australia Pty Limited
ACN 009 913 517
A member of the HarperCollins*Publishers* (Australia) Pty Limited Group

Copyright © P. Slessor 1944, 1957, 1993
© Introduction, Dennis Haskell, 1993

This book is copyright.
Apart from any fair dealing for the purposes of private study, research,
criticism or review, as permitted under the Copyright Act, no part may
be reproduced by any process without written permission.
Inquiries should be addressed to the publishers.

HarperCollins*Publishers*
Level 13, 201 Elizabeth Street, Sydney NSW 2000, Australia
31 View Road, Glenfield, Auckland 10, New Zealand
77-85 Fulham Palace Road, London W6 8JB, United Kingdom
2 Bloor Street East, 20th Floor, Toronto, Ontario M4W 1A8, Canada
10 East 53rd Street, New York NY 10032, USA

National Library of Australia Cataloguing-in-Publication data:

Slessor, K. 1901–1971.
Selected poems.
ISBN 0 207 18298 1.
I. Dennis Haskell. II. Title.
A821.3

Cover details: John Olsen, *Salute to Slessor's Five Bells* (detail)
Acrylic on plywood, 21 m x 3 m
Commissioned for the Sydney Opera House Concert Hall
Northern Foyer by the Sir William Dobell Foundation; donated 1973
Reproduced by permission of the artist and Sydney Opera House Trust
Printed in Australia by Griffin Press.

70gsm Classic used by HarperCollins*Publishers* is a natural, recyclable
product made from wood grown in sustainable forests. The manufacturing
processes conform to the environmental regulations in the country of
origin, Finland.

13 12 11   11 12 13

Beach Burial

Softly and humbly to the Gulf of Arabs
The convoys of dead sailors come;
At night they sway and wander in the
    waters far under,
But morning rolls them in the foam.

Between the sob and clubbing of the gunfire
Someone, it seems, has time for this,
To pluck them from the shallows and bury
    them in burrows
And tread the sand upon their nakedness;

And each cross, the driven stake of tidewood,
Bears the last signature of men,
Written with such perplexity, with such
    bewildered pity,
The words choke as they begin —

"Unknown seaman" — the ghostly pencil
Wavers and fades, the purple drips,
The breath of the wet season has washed
    their inscriptions
As blue as drowned men's lips.

Dead seamen, gone in search of the
    same landfall,
Whether as enemies they fought,
Or fought with us, or neither; the sand
    joins them together,
Enlisted on the other front

El Alamein, 1942

Ken Slessor

INTRODUCTION

In September 1944, while Kenneth Slessor was working as Australia's Official War Correspondent, Angus and Robertson published a selection of his work under the title *One Hundred Poems*. In 1957 Slessor added three poems and the book was republished under the simple title *Poems*. Although he lived until 1971 Slessor, who was rigorously self-critical, never published another new poem. One hundred and three poems may seem a modest output on which to base an important literary reputation but Slessor's work has been noticed by every important Australian poet since then, and *Poems* has never been out of print.

Slessor's poetry is important not only for the quality of the writing, which continues to speak to readers of eternal human concerns, but also because it is pivotal in Australia's literary history. More than any other writer, Slessor's work turned Australian literature towards the modern. The earliest poem written here is 'Marco Polo', composed in October 1920, when Slessor was just nineteen years old. It derives, as the poem's first word indicates, not from Australian life but from Slessor's reading, and is lit by the flare of his imagination:

> *... past those plaster dragon-heads,*
> *Those frescoes cut with curious flowers,*
> *In verdigris and lilac-reds*
> *Old tiles gleamed on the crusted towers,*
> *While bridges cleft of serpent-stone*
> *Bowed by their side, like branches blown*
> *From some high granite Tree of Life*
>   *Whose roots were coiled round Kublai's throne.*

Nothing like this had been written in Australia before. The gleaming density of the stanza's images, hard cut like the tiles and towers it presents, a syntax as intricate as Kublai's carvings, extensive alliteration and attention to sound patterning and shifting rhythm all point to a poetry of fascination and precision, designed to evoke not just describe. It is a long way away from the brumby-dusted tracks of Lawson and Paterson, the formal, intellectual poetry of Christopher Brennan or the drifting Celtic twilight of Victor Daley which constituted the strength of Australian poetry at the time. Even this early poem points to Slessor's lifelong concern with a 'quality of magic'[1] in poetic language, derived from a fierce attention to detail and an aesthetic of the concrete image. Language is the most abstract medium available to all the arts, a system of shapes on the page which aims to label sense-filled experience or ideas and concepts which proceed from experience. Through images Slessor tries to evoke the sensory qualities of experience and to give concepts a flesh-and-blood, lived-with 'feel'. How far Slessor could take this is shown in 'Five Bells', one of Slessor's last poems. Unquestionably one of the greatest, and perhaps *the* greatest, of all Australian poems, 'Five Bells' is a meditation on the inner and the external experiences of time, and is simultaneously an elegy for his friend Joe Lynch, who drowned in Sydney Harbour. In going over Joe's drowning, which had occurred eight years before Slessor began the poem, Slessor relives it, and he uses images to evoke the barely imaginable moment of death:

> *I felt the wet push its black thumb-balls in,*
> *The night you died, I felt your eardrums crack,*
> *And the short agony, the longer dream,*
> *The Nothing that was neither long nor short;*

But I was bound, and could not go that way,
But I was blind, and could not feel your hand.

This is the most powerful evocation of death I know of in the English language, a compression and stretching of words to depict the inexplicable. The very pressure of the writing suggests the extent of Slessor's empathy with Lynch, but enormous poignancy is generated by the simple statements that declare an inability to identify fully with his dead friend. 'Bound' in life, Slessor could not go with his. These few lines are sufficient to demonstrate the power and flexibility of Slessor's poetry.

'Marco Polo' and 'Five Bells' convey intensity of different kinds, but a fuller sense of Slessor's flexibility is revealed by considering the colloquial humour of 'A Bushranger', the indulgent languor of 'Country Towns', the melodrama of 'Wild Grapes', or the jokey sexuality of 'Lesbia's Daughter'. Slessor was also the author of some stinging satires, including section VIII, of 'The Old Play', 'Crustacean Rejoinder' and 'An Inscription for Dog River'. Most brilliant of all the satires is 'Vesper-Song of the Reverend Samuel Marsden', which portrays the powerful minister and political figure of the early Sydney colony as a sanctimonious sadist:

Lord, I have sung with ceaseless lips
A tinker's litany of whips,
. . .
My stripes of jewelled blood repeat
A scarlet Grace for holy meat.

Given its subject the 'Vesper-Song' is a distinctively Australian poem, as are 'Five Bells' with its portrayal of Sydney Harbour, 'William Street', 'A Bushranger', 'Five Visions of Captain Cook' and many other works by Slessor. Yet Slessor's poetry first gained prominence through his association with Jack and Norman Lindsay, whose philosophy was against nationalism of any sort. Slessor met the famous artist, Norman, and his bohemian, literary son Jack in the early 1920s. At the time Slessor had begun an outstanding career in journalism, writing for the Sydney *Sun* a poetic prose that had never before been seen in Australian newspapers and has never been seen since. The Lindsays disdained Australia's bush tradition as well as the Europe which had produced The Great War. Slessor joined with them in editing and publishing the magazine *Vision*, which through just four issues in 1923–24 passed judgement on many of the major figures in Western culture, consigning artists such as Dante, Raphael, Shelley, Shaw and Picasso into oblivion, while praising Rubens, Keats, Beethoven and Nietzsche. These judgements were largely the work of Jack Lindsay, and although silly they do convey one important point. Australian poetic tradition until then might be seen to have had a Colonial phase followed by a Nationalist phase. Culturally, people in a new country, as Australia was for white people from 1788 onwards, can make one of two choices: they can look back to the old country or they can look forward to the new. In Australia, they first produced a Colonial phase, in which poets saw Australia as William Charles Wentworth described it in his poem 'Australasia': 'a new Britannia in another world'. Colonial poets celebrated similarities between Australia and Britain. The second choice produced a Nationalist phase, in which poets celebrated whatever was different from Britain—the animals, the bush, the man from Snowy River. Slessor's distinctively Australian poems show his command of a sophisticated nationalism. Other poems show, as do the polemical judgements of Vision, a sense that the European heritage can belong to Australian artists without their being overawed by it; Slessor and the Lindsays did not display a cultural cringe.

The use Slessor made of that heritage introduced a new level of sophistication and modernity into Australian poetry. Slessor's family background, especially on his father's side, helped in this regard. Slessor's family name was actually 'Schloesser', until his father changed it when World War I broke out in 1914. Kenneth was thirteen at the time, and was descended from a notable line of German musicians. His father had been born in England and had undertaken university studies in Liège, Belgium; his children had to speak French at breakfast or else they weren't allowed to eat. Kenneth Slessor's assimilation of Europe is apparent in his sophisticated poetic techniques and also, more obviously, in the subject matter of poems such as 'Nuremberg', which deals with Albrecht Dürer, 'Heine in Paris', which presents the last hours of the German poet Heinrich Heine, and 'La Dame du Palais de la Reine'. European sophistication meant that Slessor in poems like 'Crow Country', 'Talbingo' and 'South Country' could treat Australian landscape in ways that were unimaginable before he wrote, and paved the way for novels such as Patrick White's *Voss* and Randolph Stow's *To the Islands*. 'After the whey-faced anonymity/Of river-gums and scribbly-gums and bush' you reach the farms of the south country 'As if the argument of trees were done'. This is not only brilliantly descriptive writing, it is an observation of the landscape with more thought than it had been given before. Slessor presents the landscape not as if it were simply there, but with an awareness that it is only there meaningfully in being perceived. A landscape of 'whey-faced anonymity' is clearly a landscape as interpreted by an individual mind. What is presented is an interaction between landscape and mind, between outer reality and inner reality, so that the poem is as much about the mind's hesitations and fears as it is about the country south of Sydney.

'Heine in Paris' presents a dying Heine, and death is a strong presence in Slessor's work. Death is there from early work to late; it hovers around the early poem 'Mangroves', is the allegorical subject in 'The Night-Ride' and 'Next Turn', and provides the explicit subject of 'Five Bells' and 'Beach Burial'. Slessor's concern throughout is not with the pain of dying but with the metaphysical nothingness that death represents for those who have no faith in an afterlife. 'The Old Play' presents a wide range of gods from various cultures, and its last section describes them as 'Made out of nothing/By men's minds'. Slessor is the sort of person who, in the poem 'Stars', can look at the night sky and find that his strongest awareness is not of the stars but of the 'black cups of space' between them, 'those tunnels of nothingness'. This poet whose lines are so informed by sensory awareness, saw death as the annihilation of the senses, and infinity as a 'trap-door, eternal and merciless'.

Death is linked to that other theme which seems almost pervasive in Slessor's poetry: time. 'Five Bells' relives the life of Joe Lynch within approximately three seconds, and contrasts the inner, subjective experience of time with time as measured by the '*fidget wheels*' of clocks. In 'Nuremberg', the very first poem in the book to be published, we look down on Albrecht Dürer (1471–1528) at work, in a room where 'Clocks had been bolted out, the flux of years/Defied'. Slessor's most extended treatment of the theme comes in 'Out of Time', which reveals how lyrical his work can be. Slessor's beloved Sydney Harbour provides the context and imagery for this interwoven trio of sonnets. The poem meshes intellectual and imagistic thought as Time, 'the hundred yachts', 'the wave', 'the bony knife' provides illusions of an eternal moment and of a type of consciousness beyond that of normal human life. The bluntness of the poem's closing rhyme shows that this is illusion: we can imagine ourselves 'out of Time' but cannot live there.

What can live there is Slessor's poetry, seemingly richer with every passing year. Slessor's interests in history, in Australian and international culture, in music, in maps, his fascination with Sydney and its harbour, his sense of humour and his originality provide a great sweep in the range of his poems, even though his total output was small. Slessor stopped writing poetry more than thirty years before he died, in 1971. It was during these years of poetic silence that he wrote 'Some Notes on the Poems' which are reprinted in this edition. Slessor's 'Notes' are modest, direct and uncomplicated; amongst other things they reveal how far from a Slessor poem's full meaning is any prose explanation. No one who has put pen to paper in Australia has ever had a stronger sense of the meaningfulness of rhythm, music and sound in language than Slessor. Perhaps the stringent demands of his meticulously crafted work encouraged him to stop writing early; in an essay of 1947 Slessor described writing poetry as a pleasure but as 'a pleasure out of hell' [2]. But before he stopped, 'from clods of aching thought' ('The Knife') Slessor turned up many of the sharpest poems in Australian literature.

DENNIS HASKELL
Perth, 1993

1. 'The Quality of Magic', in *Kenneth Slessor*, ed. Dennis Haskell, St Lucia: University of Queensland Press, 1991, p168
2. 'Writing Poetry: The Why and the How', in *Kenneth Slessor*, ed. Dennis Haskell, p. 162.

CONTENTS

	PAGE
Introduction	iv
Earth-Visitors	1
Nuremberg	3
Pan at Lane Cove	4
Taoist	6
Rubens' Innocents	7
Marco Polo	8
Chessmen	10
Mangroves	11
Thief of the Moon	12
Heine in Paris	13
Winter Dawn	17
A Surrender	18
The Man of Sentiment, Part One	19
The Man of Sentiment, Part Two	25
Thieves' Kitchen	32
Stars	33
The Ghost	34
Undine	35
Next Turn	36
City Nightfall	37
Adventure Bay	38
The Night-Ride	39
A Sunset	39
Realities	40

		PAGE
Music		42
(i) Music, on the air's edge, rides alone		42
(ii) A ship in hell marooned		42
(iii) O, silent night, dark beach		43
(iv) In the pans of straw-coned country		44
(v) In and out the countryfolk		44
(vi) Torches and running fire; the flagstones drip		45
(vii) In the apple-country, in the apple-trees		46
(viii) Open! It is the moon knocking with fists of air		46
(ix) Once, at your words, I would have struck to flame		47
(x) Nothing grows on the stone trees		48
(xi) Come in your painted coaches, friends of mine		49
(xii) Look up! Thou hast a shining Guest		50
Captain Dobbin		51
The Atlas		56
(i) The King of Cuckooz		56
(ii) Post-Roads		58
(iii) Dutch Seacoast		59
(iv) Mermaids		60
(v) The Seafight		62
To Myself		64
Elegy in a Botanic Gardens		65
Trade Circular		66
Five Visions of Captain Cook		67
(i) Cook was a captain of the Admiralty		67
(ii) Flowers turned to stone		68
(iii) Two chronometers the captain had		69
(iv) Sometimes the god would fold his wings		70
(v) After the candles had gone out		71

Wild Grapes	74
La Dame du Palais de la Reine	75
Waters	76
Glubbdubdrib	77
Rubens' Hell	79
Burying Friends	81
Crow Country	82
Serenade	82
Talbingo	83
Country Towns	84
A Bushranger	85
Gulliver	86
Fixed Ideas	87
The Country Ride	88
The Nabob	90
Toilet of a Dandy	91
Metempsychosis	92
Mephistopheles Perverted	93
The Old Play	94
(i) In an old play-house, in an old play	94
(ii) In the old play-house, in the watery flare	94
(iii) Marduk his jewelled finger flips	95
(iv) But who are we to sneer	95
(v) And who are we to argue with our lutes	96
(vi) Camazotz and Anubis	97
(vii) "Shang Ya! I want to be your friend"	98
(viii) This is really a Complete Life and Works	99
(ix) A bird sang in the jaws of night	100
(x) My strings I break, my breast I beat	101
(xi) But Life we know, but Life we know	101
(xii) You that we raised	102

	PAGE
Crustacean Rejoinder	103
Out of Time	104
(i) I saw Time flowing like the hundred yachts	104
(ii) Time leaves the lovely moment at his back	104
(iii) Leaning against the golden undertow	105
Sleep	106
Sensuality	107
Lesbia's Daughter	108
The Knife	109
Cock-Crow	110
North Country	111
South Country	112
Last Trams	113
(i) That street washed with violet	113
(ii) Then, from the skeletons of trams	113
Advice to Psychologists	114
Vesper-Song of the Reverend Samuel Marsden	115
To a Friend	116
William Street	117
Cannibal Street	118
To the Poetry of Hugh McCrae	119
Full Orchestra	120
Five Bells	121
Polarities	125
An Inscription for Dog River	126
Beach Burial	127
Some Notes on the Poems	128
Index to first lines	141

EARTH-VISITORS
(*To N.L.*)

THERE were strange riders once, came gusting down
Cloaked in dark furs, with faces grave and sweet,
And white as air. None knew them, they were strangers—
Princes gone feasting, barons with gipsy eyes
And names that rang like viols—perchance, who knows,
Kings of old Tartary, forgotten, swept from Asia,
Blown on raven chargers across the world,
For ever smiling sadly in their beards
    And stamping abruptly into courtyards at midnight.

Post-boys would run, lanterns hang frostily, horses fume,
The strangers wake the Inn. Men, staring outside
Past watery glass, thick panes, could watch them eat,
Dyed with gold vapours in the candleflame,
Clapping their gloves, and stuck with crusted stones,
Their garments foreign, their talk a strange tongue,
    But sweet as pineapple—it was Archdukes, they must be.

In daylight, nothing; only their prints remained
Bitten in snow. They'd gone, no one knew where,
Or when, or by what road—no one could guess—
None but some sleepy girls, half tangled in dreams,
Mixing up miracle and desire; laughing, at first,
Then staring with bright eyes at their beds, opening their
    lips,
Plucking a crushed gold feather in their fingers,
And laughing again, eyes closed. But one remembered,
Between strange kisses and cambric, in the dark,
That unearthly beard had lifted.... "Your name, child?"
"Sophia, sir—and what to call your Grace?"
    Like a bubble of gilt, he had laughed "Mercury!"

It is long now since great daemons walked on earth,
Staining with wild radiance a country bed,
And leaving only a confusion of sharp dreams
To vex a farm-girl—that, and perhaps a feather,
Some thread of the Cloth of Gold, a scale of metal,
Caught in her hair. The unpastured Gods have gone,
They are above those fiery-coasted clouds
Floating like fins of stone in the burnt air,
And earth is only a troubled thought to them
That sometimes drifts like wind across the bodies
   Of the sky's women.

There is one yet comes knocking in the night,
The drums of sweet conspiracy on the pane,
When darkness has arched his hands over the bush
And Springwood steams with dew, and the stars look down
On that one lonely chamber....
She is there suddenly, lit by no torch or moon,
But by the shining of her naked body.
Her breasts are berries broken in snow; her hair
Blows in a gold rain over and over them.
She flings her kisses like warm guineas of love,
   And when she walks, the stars walk with her above.

She knocks. The door swings open, shuts again.
"Your name, child?"
   A thousand birds cry "Venus!"

NUREMBERG

So quiet it was in that high, sun-steeped room,
So warm and still, that sometimes with the light
Through the great windows, bright with bottle-panes,
There'd float a chime from clock-jacks out of sight,
    Clapping iron mallets on green copper gongs.

But only in blown music from the town's
Quaint horologue could Time intrude ... you'd say
Clocks had been bolted out, the flux of years
Defied, and that high chamber sealed away
    From earthly change by some old alchemist.

And, oh, those thousand towers of Nuremberg
Flowering like leaden trees outside the panes:
Those gabled roofs with smoking cowls, and those
Encrusted spires of stone, those golden vanes
    On shining housetops paved with scarlet tiles!

And all day nine wrought-pewter manticores
Blinked from their spouting faucets, not five steps
Across the cobbled street, or, peering through
The rounds of glass, espied that sun-flushed room
    With Dürer graving at intaglios.

O happy nine, spouting your dew all day
In green-scaled rows of metal, whilst the town
Moves peacefully below in quiet joy....
O happy gargoyles to be gazing down
    On Albrecht Dürer and his plates of iron!

PAN AT LANE COVE

SCALY with poison, bright with flame,
Great fungi steam beside the gate,
Run tentacles through flagstone cracks,
Or claw beyond, where meditate
Wet poplars on a pitchy lawn.
Some seignior of colonial fame
Has planted here a stone-cut faun
    Whose flute juts like a frozen flame.

O lonely faun, what songs are these
For skies where no Immortals hide?
Why finger in this dour abode
Those Pan-pipes girdled at your side?
Your Gods, and Hellas too, have passed,
Forsaken are the Cyclades,
And surely, faun, you are the last
    To pipe such ancient songs as these.

Yet, blow your stone-lipped flute and blow
Those red-and-silver pipes of Pan.
Cold stars are bubbling round the moon,
Which, like some golden Indiaman
Disgorged by waterspouts and blown
Through heaven's archipelago,
Drives orange bows by clouds of stone . . .
    Blow, blow your flute, you stone boy, blow!

And, Chiron, pipe your centaurs out,
The night has looped a smoky scarf
Round campanili in the town,
And thrown a cloak about Clontarf.

Now earth is ripe for Pan again,
Barbaric ways and Paynim rout,
And revels of old Samian men.
   O Chiron, pipe your centaurs out.

This garden by the dark Lane Cove
Shall spark before thy music dies
With silver sandals; all thy gods
Be conjured from Ionian skies.
Those poplars in a fluting-trice
They'll charm into an olive-grove
And dance a while in Paradise
   Like men of fire above Lane Cove.

TAOIST

THOSE friends of Lao-Tzu, those wise old men
Dozing all day in lemon-silken robes,
With tomes of beaten jade spread knee to knee,
And pipe-stem, shining cold with silver, poised
In steaming play, and still a finger free
   To dog the path of some forgotten pen;

Almost their bee-sweet ancient words incline
My mind to those old pagan ways, beloved
By mandarins and mages, now but dust
In drowsy pyramids. What creed is this,
Save that which those philosophers discussed
   In gold pavilions, over musky wine?

> *"Repenting always of forgotten wrongs*
> *Will never bring thy heart to rest, for thought*
> *Repairs no whit of evil; rather cast*
> *Thy meditations in that utter void*
> *To which all human deeds resolve at last...."*

So runs the burden of their thousand songs.

Here, in this dark Star-Chamber of the soul,
You stand arraigned, O slayer of my heart...
But I am tired of hoarding up the grist
Of anger, and remember Lao-Tzu.
Revenge is empty to the Taoist,
   And tears of penitence a futile toll!

RUBENS' INNOCENTS

If all those tumbling babes of heaven,
    Plump cherubim with blown cheeks,
Could vault in these warm skies, or leaven
    Our starry silent mountain-peaks—
O painter of chub-faced, shining-thighed
    Fat Ganymedes of God—what noise
Would churn between the clouds and stride
    Far downward from those rose-mouthed boys!

Down to our spires their lusty whooping,
    Fanfares of Paradise, would speed,
Far down to dark-faced clergy stooping
    Round altars of their doleful creed;
And God, whose wings of silver sweep
    Like metal afire on heaven's rim,
Would daze them with a twinkling peep
    Of those young moon-stained cherubim—

Then, for a trice, their skies might sparkle,
    And some gold ichor splash amid
Those most respectable, patriarchal
    Purveyors of stale pardons, hid
Behind their old cathedral closes
    From this unguessed, unguessable God,
Shining before their learned noses
    Down roads that Peter Rubens trod.

MARCO POLO

Reading how Marco Polo came
By bridle-path to Kanbalu,
Forgotten fibres wake to flame,
And smoke old memories anew....
For in a bygone life of mine
I watched the carven rampart shine,
Where Kublai's five-clawed dragons glowed
    Like painted wyverns, line on line.

And past those plaster dragon-heads,
Those frescoes cut with curious flowers,
In verdigris and lilac-reds
Old tiles gleamed on the crusted towers,
While bridges cleft of serpent-stone
Bowed by their side, like branches blown
From some high granite Tree of Life
    Whose roots were coiled round Kublai's throne.

O myrtles on the Jasper Mount,
O forest-towered elephants,
And fire-fish in the topaz fount
With red fins blown like water-plants,
And green cornelian tortoise-rows
Below the aqueduct, and those
Gold-feathered cranes, I saw them all,
    How many ages gone, who knows?

I saw tall gilded Tartars pass
Behind their marble balustrades,
With maces made of beaten brass
And turquoise-hafted sabre-blades.

I heard the little golden bells
Blow faintly down the citadels,
And spied those ivory courts within
    Through windows of transparent shells.

But past the fountain-pools I peered,
Beyond the birds, to that divan,
Where, fingering his tawny beard,
In silence dreamed the splendid Khan.
Green china bowls of wine were there,
And oranges and milk-of-mare,
While, stamping on his jewelled wrist,
    A falcon climbed with eyes aflare.

He's gone; and with him, flowers and birds,
And old Venetians too, have died;
Yet burnt in Marco Polo's words,
Those unforgotten splendours hide . . .
And, tired of life's new-fashioned plan,
I long to be barbarian.
I'm sick of modern men, I wish
    You were still living, Kublai-Khan!

CHESSMEN

CHAFING on flags of ebony and pearl,
   My paladins are waiting. Loops of smoke
Stoop slowly from the coffee-cups, and curl
   In thin fantastic patterns down the room
By cabinets of chinaware, to whirl
   With milk-blue tobacco-steam, and fume
Together past our pipes, outside the door.

Soon may we lounge in silence, O my friend,
   Behind those carven men-at-arms of chess
Dyed coral-red with dragon's blood, and spend
   The night with noiseless warfare. Queens and rooks
With chiselled ivory warriors must contend
   And counter-plots from old Arabian books
Be conjured to the march of knights and pawns.

MANGROVES

These black bush-waters, heavy with crusted boughs
  Like plumes above dead captains, wake the mind. . . .
Uncounted kissing, unremembered vows,
  Nights long forgotten, moons too dark to find,
Or stars too cold . . . all quick things that have fled
  Whilst these old bubbles uprise in older stone,
Return like pale dead faces of children dead,
  Staring unfelt through doors for ever unknown.

O silent ones that drink these timeless pools,
  Eternal brothers, bending so deeply over,
Your branches tremble above my tears again . . .
  And even my songs are stolen from some old lover
Who cried beneath your leaves like other fools,
  While still they whisper "in vain . . . in vain . . . in vain . . ."

THIEF OF THE MOON

Thief of the moon, thou robber of old delight,
Thy charms have stolen the star-gold, quenched the moon—
Cold, cold are the birds that, bubbling out of night,
Cried once to my ears their unremembered tune—
Dark are those orchards, their leaves no longer shine,
No orange's gold is globed like moonrise there—
O thief of the earth's old loveliness, once mine,
    Why dost thou waste all beauty to make thee fair?

Break, break thy strings, thou lutanists of earth,
Thy musics touch me not—let midnight cover
With pitchy seas those leaves of orange and lime,
I'll not repent. The world's no longer worth
One smile from thee, dear pirate of place and time,
    Thief of old loves that haunted once thy lover!

HEINE IN PARIS

LATE: a cold smear of sunlight bathes the room;
    The gilt lime of winter, a sun grown melancholy old,
Streams in the glass. Outside, ten thousand chimneys fume,
    Looping the weather-birds with rings of gold;
The spires of Paris, pricked in an iron spume,
    Uprise like stars of water, and mail the sky.
Night comes: the wind is cold.

La Mouche has lit the candles, cleared up the mess.
    She is talking, this merry little girl, of the new clown,
Mercutio in red spots, and Miss Nellie, the Equine Princess,
    Who can ride three terrible horses upside-down....
"*Mon dieu, quelle cirque!*"... and Madame Stephanie's dress..
    "As true as I live"... the clear little voice trickles on,
All over the Circus, on and on, and all over the town.

Now she has creaked downstairs. Heine is left alone,
    Knees hugged in bed, the drug purring in his brain,
And the windows turning blue. He can see some clouds being blown,
    Scraping their big, soft bellies on the pane:
"Take me, O Clouds!"—but in a puff they've flown.
    So once they fled in *Eighteen Twenty-Nine*
From—Hamburg, was it?—in a damp disdain....

Hamburg—those roofs of tulip-red, those floating trees,
    Those black masts clotting the air, and swart cigars,
And puffed old bankers panting along the quays,
    And Uncle Solomon shouting amongst the spars,
And Uncle Solomon's cargoes, coffee and cheese,
    And Uncle Solomon's face, like a copper moon,
And Uncle Solomon's daughter, and the stars, the stars.

O, Hamburg and Amalie—the stars and dung—
   He remembered suddenly that night he stood below,
Dark in the street, with stinging heart and helpless tongue,
   And her face passed in the pane, like paper to and fro.
But in a thousand songs that song was never sung.
   Amalie, Amalie, who was only a foaming of thought,
A thing thought of, and forgotten, long ago.

And Louise, Diana, and Jenny, and all those bright,
   Mad girls who had scrawled their names inside his mind—
All vanished, all gone; and all of them forged in a night,
   Conspired of dreams, and leaving no dream behind,
Ungrateful for their dreaming—flight after flight
   Of musings wrapped in satin, fancies in silk,
   And a thousand thoughts of naked roses and milk,
By love and the moon designed.

But now it seemed that these were only one thought,
   One stone of Venus, cut with a hundred sides,
One girl revealed ten thousand times, and caught
   Ten thousand times from out those amorous tides.
Now she was gone. They were all gone, those girls that he had sought,
   All gone, or paunched in marriage, or crushed in graves,
Or promised for other men's brides.

And it was only a ghost's hair that had spilt,
   Fur of the night, in kissing dark and strange,
To choke his lips. And all of those worlds he'd built,
   The girls he'd conjured before his dreams took mange,
The rogues he'd stamped on, harlot, trollop, and jilt,
   The fools he'd blistered—all of them passed and forgotten;
But that—*that* did not change.

Men crumbled, man lived on. In that animal's face,
   'Twas but a squirt aimed at the moon, to fling contempt.
Meyerbeer, Borne, and Klopstock vanished, but in their place
   New Klopstocks, Meyerbeers blown again, and Bornes undreamt,
Sprang up like fungi, and there remained no trace
   Of lashings past. Men, men he could flog for ever,
But man was still exempt.

That did not change—always the world remained,
   Breathing and sleeping; loving and taking in love;
Fighting and coupling; life by the belly constrained,
   Stupid in roads of flesh; eating, but never enough;
Ravening, never to cease; warring, but nothing gained;
   Babbling to silent Christs; climbing to heavens of the brain
Unknown, unanswering, above.

All these remained, words passed. The paper he'd filled,
   Deep to the lips in bitter salt, with fury and tears,
No man remembered; anger and fools were stilled
   In dust alike—and out of those roaring years,
What now was left of all the passion he'd spilled,
   The fire he'd struck? A cadence or two of love,
A song that had stroked men's ears.

All wrong, all wasted. Now, in this winter snow,
   In the black winds from Russia, and the printed mane of night,
Heine looked out, and gazed at the world below,
   Thick with old chemicals, breaking far out of sight
With ageless tides of man—ah, granite flow,
   Eternal, changeless flux of humanity,
Undying darkness and light!

Not treading those floods could save him—not striking stone,
 Not damning the world could serve—only to fly,
Careless of men and their shouting—untouched—alone—
 Snatched by his own gods from a falling sky,
And singing his own way—clutching his own, his own,
 Blind to the world—yes, that was the road of Heine—
Up to the sun, solitary, a speck in the ether—

"Ha, now, Christ Jesus and Jehovah, I choose to die!"

WINTER DAWN

At five I wake, rise, rub on the smoking pane
A port to see—water breathing in the air,
Boughs broken. The sun comes up in a golden stain,
Floats like a glassy sea-fruit. There is mist everywhere,
White and humid, and the Harbour is like plated stone,
Dull flakes of ice. One light drips out alone,
One bead of winter-red, smouldering in the steam,
Quietly over the roof-tops—another window
Touched with a crystal fire in the sun's gullies,
One lonely star of the morning, where no stars gleam.

Far away on the rim of this great misty cup,
The sun gilds the dead suburbs as he rises up,
Diamonds the wind-cocks, makes glitter the crusted spikes
On moss-drowned gables. Now the tiles drip scarlet-wet,
Swim like birds' paving-stones, and sunlight strikes
Their watery mirrors with a moister rivulet,
Acid and cold. Here lie those mummied Kings,
Men sleeping in houses, embalmed in stony coffins,
Till the Last Trumpet calls their galleries up,
And the suburbs rise with distant murmurings.

O buried dolls, O men sleeping invisible there,
I stare above your mounds of stone, lean down,
Marooned and lonely in this bitter air,
And in one moment deny your frozen town,
Renounce your bodies—earth falls in clouds away,
Stones lose their meaning, substance is lost in clay,
Roofs fade, and that small smoking forgotten heap,
The city, dissolves to a shell of bricks and paper,
Empty, without purpose, a thing not comprehended,
A broken tomb, where ghosts unknown sleep.

And the least crystal weed, shaken with frost,
The furred herbs of silver, the daisies round-eyed and tart,
Painted in antic china, the smallest night-flower tossed
Like a bright penny on the lawn, stirs more my heart.
Strikes deeper this morning air, than mortal towers
Dried to a common blindness, fainter than flowers,
Fordone, extinguished, as the vapours break,
And dead in the dawn. O Sun that kills with life,
And brings to breath all silent things—O Dawn,
Waken me with old earth, keep me awake!

A SURRENDER

When to those Venusbergs, thy breasts,
By wars of love and moonlight batteries,
My lips have stormed—O pout thy mouth above,
Lean down those culverins twain, and bid me spike
Their bells with kissing, and their powder steal,
And by night-marches take their garrisons—
No blood shall stain those battlefields of lace
But all their snows run dappled with deep roses,
And thou, I trow, sweet enemy of love,
    Shalt find a conquest in capitulation!

THE MAN OF SENTIMENT

Part One

[A walled garden of York. It is an August Sunday, and the baying of deep church-bells is blown faintly in a warm wind. Laurence Sterne, prebendary, aged forty-six, and Catherine de Fromantel, a girl who sings at Ranelagh, are dawdling through the arbours, and pause at a path which runs between hedges and cypress-trees round a corner some fifty yards away. Catherine has walked down such a path before, it is to be feared, and halts cautiously upon its fringes.]

LAURENCE: Nay, 'tis no Devil's walk,
It leads to what? Some leaden Child with lips
Blown open, spouting fountain-dew on birds
That drowsily dive the pool ... some secret Lawn
Tight locked away in mazes, and trod by none
Save one old crazy Gardener ... aye, 'tis prick'd
In curious inks on charts of old, I'll vow,
Drown'd in some careless Viscount's library
Five hundred years, and like to rot five more.
Now we, my child, wait idly, toe to brink,
Whilst I must pray thee to walk hand-in-hand
Not fifty steps along a sanded alley....

CATHERINE: Such paths have led to dangerous lands before,
And many a maid's marched less than fifty steps
To-day no maiden ... 'tis a well-known Grove,
Thy maze of lime and bergamot, good priest
...

	Plump Notaries would buzz with ivory tablets,
	Plaguing the round-tubb'd orange-trees to blab
	Could they but speak.... Oh, trust me, sir, I know
	Those leafy Rogues too well!
LAURENCE:	Nay, Kit, these trees
	Are stout duennas, this garden a Dutch garden,
	And sure the grass would rust to yellow stalks
	If lovers betray'd its beaded innocence.
	Come ... seven steps ... I'll swear to coax no more....
	As far as the Cypress ... not a bee's foot further....
	As far as the Cypress....
CATHERINE:	No, I tell you, no!
	(*She allows herself to be led a few steps.*)
LAURENCE:	But here the spices of some little trees,
	And certain hot, heavy orchard-essences
	From fruits that have molten in their leaves, do tell
	Stupendous tales of Paddocks round the turn—
	Flat, knee-thick fields of laziness, piping all day
	With flies and ants, and most bewhisker'd Bees—
	Great solemn Bees, too plump to take a flower
	Because their weight might shake the petals down—
CATHERINE:	Lord, where's the maze, and little carven Lad
	He—nay, I will not—nay, sir—fie, a priest,
	A prebendary wrestling with a wench
	Who's like as not to quaver in dark Taverns—
	Oh, sir, have done!

LAURENCE: Now here's a mystery—
She'll dawdle from *St. Michael's* with you, walk
With prinking flutters past the choristers,
And take the turnpike, handed by a priest,
But let that saintly gentleman divert
Her footsteps from the vulgar throng, to grant her
Five hundred feet of private ambulation—
Oh, no—those lanes of lime-trees tempt her not—
She'll turn for home!

CATHERINE: You know it's not the lanes,
Nor lime-trees either that I like not—priests
Are sable Eunuchs in the public streets,
But passionate rascals in an orangery!

LAURENCE: Passion? You tease me, Kit—I keep no passion
In these quiet deeps of Yorkshire—no, and passion
Runs not in veins that time and the church have froze
To pipes of ancient lead—ha, passion, ha, ha!
This torn Divine accus'd of gallantry!
No doubt, a charge of attempted defloration
Of nuns past counting in the convent close
Would next have been preferr'd, if my religion
Had but agreed with that of the old ladies!
"*Alas, poor Yorick—here lies a three-nun man,*"
I thank you for the compliment, dear Slut,
But Love's a dissipation I'm denied—
My reasons are innumerable, chief amongst them
The fact that it disorders my digestion,
And also—most important—I'm a disciple
Of that delicious old philosophy

             Which flings us womankind to prime and dandle
             And dog forever in the name of *Plato*—
             Yes, I—I'm a Platonic—and our friendship
             Mere rubbing of dim, spiritual flanks
             As legally prescribed in the Symposium. . . .
             'Tis writ, I warrant you, in authentic Greek,
             And must disarm all scruples.

CATHERINE: I'm no scholar,
             And Greek's but Greek. The body's been my school,
             Gilding it, dusting its rounds with Orris-root,
             Waxing its lips and silencing its cries—
             In Greek I'm lacking, but it seems to me
             That when a lad stands tugging a maiden's waist
             Near snapping a Lace that oughtn't to be snapp'd—
             He may quote *Plato*, but his bent's the same.

LAURENCE: 'Tis monstrous wrong! I'll swear no bones of mine
             Have taboured it to Love—or if they have
             They've groaned like skeletons in *Holbein's* Dance—
             Aye, creaked and jarred with miserable joy
             To cheerless ends. I'm no Voluptary
             New-greased with Love's pomatum—look at me,
             My name's the Reverend *Tristram* . . . *Laurie Sterne* . . .
             Or *Yorick*, as you like . . . aged in the suburbs
             Of thirty-five or thereabouts . . . gaunt, long-legged,
             Peruked grotesquely on the north-west border
             With powdered wool, a trifle disarranged.

>Poor *Tristram* ... all he quests are cast-off things,
>A smile tossed like a cherry to the birds,
>The casual brush of eyes across a Counter,
>Some careless touch of skin like flutter'd silk,
>Or sweet munificence of Beauty thrown
>Like pennies to the Post-boy ... secret breasts
>Like ivory fruits, unbared a bending-trice
>Whilst *Janatone* leans over apricocks
>To bite their stalks off ... aye, and silken knees
>Reveal'd in twinkling foams of Dimity
>When Libertine winds run under maidens' Frocks—
>And when those Frocks are tugg'd, small naked shoulders
>That suddenly rise from ruffs of Mechlin lace,
>Veined with sly, riotous roses, then subside
>In quicksands of wild Satin and bubbling Silk
>. . .
>Poor *Tristam* ... all he seeks are these, but Life
>Bequeaths him only Sorrows. . . .
>Do you call it weak to have one's eyes brimmed up
>With tears of pity ... an ye do, I'm weak. . . .

CATHERINE: Tears, Master *Laurence*?

LAURENCE: I weep internally.
Taunt me not, Kit, my heart is old and broken.

CATHERINE: But wherefore tears?

LAURENCE: They rise like stones of crystal,
And whence they come, who knows? Perchance my Wife!

CATHERINE: Poor man—she's fast in France—

LAURENCE: Her deeds remain.
Oh, pity me, sweet child, I need thy tears.

CATHERINE: Come, let me take thee to this bench of stone,
I would thy heart were happier—

LAURENCE: Nay, not here—
'Tis cold—and there's a mound of twisted flowers
Beyond the turn, five paces past the Fish-pond,
Would net no less than two, no more than one,
In most prodigious comfort—

CATHERINE: Poor, poor *Yorick*,
I'll dab thy tears upon my petticoat. . . .

LAURENCE: Delightful Girl!

CATHERINE: Nay, wait sir,—wait, sir—O!
(They are heard talking for a while behind the corner hedge.)

THE MAN OF SENTIMENT
Part Two

[*Meard's Court, Soho. An August nightfall, 1760. Catherine is seated at a small pianoforte, Catherine's mother is examining the contents of a chest. "Tristram Shandy" has plunged Sterne into the drawing-rooms of London, and Catherine has followed.*]

MOTHER: Ten bottles of Calcavillo . . . one pot of Honey . . .
A jar of Comfits—(*sniffs*)—some Eau de Chypre . . .
The phial's of Crystal—(*sniffs*)—some few dead Posies . . .
Fourteen Epistles, dabbed with gilded sand
And sealed with crusts of lilac wax beneath . . .
Three sheets of music . . . boughpots filled with flowers . . .
Cards for the *Fête Aqueuse*. . . . O, monstrous fine!
A mirror of Bronze (I doubt its but some favour
From a Cotillon). . . . Fans, they're from the Ball. . . .
A print by *Mr. Campbell*, with Lions' Heads,
And "*STERNE*" surmounted by a loop of Roses,
Most witching smart . . . a frame of Chinese lacker
To hold th' engraving fast . . . romantic truly!
Your priest's a garter'd nobleman, and leaks
Prodigious generosity . . . in faith,
He's monstrous kind . . . aye, look you, in a fortnight

>   Full fifty-seven gifts he hath despatch'd
>   In various paquets ... aye, and written to boot
>   One hundred pages Quarto ... there's a man
>   I call of true nobility ... though, in faith,
>   He's come no closer than scroll'd Signatures
>   For thirteen weeks ... no doubt he's held in leash
>   By Satin thongs to some Duchess ... 'tis hard,
>   I do protest, to interrupt a Rout
>   With kissing girls in Soho....

CATHERINE: Light the candles,
And leave me, an you love me.

MOTHER: Aye, 'tis true
I love you, Kit. Priests do no more than that,
And *Laurie Sterne* no—

CATHERINE: Peace! Have done. I'm tired.

MOTHER: Ah, *Catherine*, you've played the trick too well
For scolding—see to it, child, I pray
That York's not drown'd in town, nor *Yorick* either.
Those red-heel'd Ladies cage him in their Hoops
Whilst he indites Epistles to *"Dear Kitty"*—
He's but a tearful babe, and may be drawn
By aught of the turns you know—a Stocking's top
Rimm'd with quick flesh—some string across the shoulder
Slipp'd from the bodice—aye, or peeps of Lace
Would snare that heart which flaps inconstantly
Like lanthorns in great Winds—

CATHERINE: Leave me, I'm tired.
(Exit Mother. Catherine plays slowly, and meanwhile Sterne enters and listens in the darkness of the door).

LAURENCE: Oh, Kit!

CATHERINE: Who's that?

LAURENCE: A wretched Gentleman,
Once known in York, now lost in London's ways.

CATHERINE: 'Tis—oh, you fright me—

LAURENCE: 'Tis but wretched *Yorick*,
Sad *Tristram*—

CATHERINE: Bring you news of that poor Priest?
'Tis many a week since last I heard of him,
And being a trifle concern'd in his success,
Pray speak of him—he's near forgotten here,
And might be dead—

LAURENCE: She jests—but Kit, I love you!

CATHERINE: "*Dear Kit—I love you—Laurence.*" So 'tis said
In fifty-seven manners, wrote with flourishes
In that poor Priest's extensive correspondence.

LAURENCE: Nay, Kit—I love you—not a moment longer
Could aught of Business, Authorship or Rank
Imprison me in cold Pall Mall—I love you!

CATHERINE: 'Tis a moment then too late. I love not you!

LAURENCE: Nay, I protest you tease me. O, *Catherine*
Have you no heart for pity—

CATHERINE: What, more pity?
Yea, miserable wretch, I grieve for you—
By *Plato*, I commiserate your woes—
Poor *Tristram*, doom'd to everlasting Routs,
Meshed in Ridottos, pent in *Fêtes Champêtres*—
O, yes, by heaven, I sympathise indeed!

LAURENCE: You mock me. 'Tis unworthy, Kit. I'll vow
No lover has danced in town more wretchedly
Than I at Carlton House—my jaws were wet—
I'll swear were wet with weeping . . . night by night
I'd steal by candlelight from Dukes and Barons,
Climb to my Room, and consecrate sad hours
To dreams of thee. . . .

CATHERINE: O, *Laurence*, come away. . . .
Back, back to Yorkshire. 'Tis a year this morning
Since that hot day in August—do you remember?

LAURENCE: Yes, I remember. 'Twas a day like this,
I rowed thee down by Ouse. . . . O, happy Boat!

CATHERINE: Nay, 'tis in vain. You know not what I mean.
No lovers pace those hedges now, the Garden
Sleeps once again. . . .

LAURENCE: Ah, heavens, the Garden, Kit!
Nay, I protest I do remember. . . .

CATHERINE: You!
Nay, you remember *Plato* and your tears,
Plato and your digestion. . . .

LAURENCE: Heavens, yes, *Plato*,
My sweet Platonic. . . .

CATHERINE: Sure the philosophy
Affords more true delight to its professor
Than to the obedient novice. Nay, 'tis vain.
I love you not . . . no, not if you coached home
And fee'd the Gods to pipe in Yorkshire gardens.

LAURENCE: *Catherine!*

CATHERINE: Nay
LAURENCE: O *Catherine*, I'll repent—
By heaven, I'll swear to post away instanter.
Run back with me to that one leaden Child
Whose cheeks were blown in smiles above our bed,
Sweet Kit of the Garden—aye, the pool drips now,
The fountain spouts again, the birds dive under,
That August morn returns—return thou with it!
CATHERINE: Oh, leave—oh, leave—
LAURENCE: Ah, *Catherine*, I love you.
Doubt me not, sweet, 'tis true. I've proved that vow
Too often since last August—aye and more,
I've naught but misery in London—fame
Hath little delight for lovers—Balls and Routs
Without your voice resolve to mere mechanics.
Believe me, Kit, I stop but long enough
To foster my luck—and with thine aid, sweet Child,
Poor *Laurence Sterne*, the rustic priest, shall swim,
Thee on his shoulders, down the gutter of Time.
CATHERINE: I would your—oh, 'tis vain—leave me, I beg.
LAURENCE: No, no. I love you!
CATHERINE: Nay, you love me not.
You love your Wife.
LAURENCE: That fume of a woman! No!
CATHERINE: You love no woman, *Tristram*—nay, no woman.

You love but Eyes whose lakes of darkness mirror
Poor *Laurence Sterne*—you love but Ears whose mazes
Resound with *Yorick's* words, and blow them back
To *Yorick* himself—you love but Lips that know
Sweet means of kissing *Yorick*, and since all lips
Accomplish kissing, in faith, you love all lips,
And most your own. Aye, Sir, you're true enough
In your own manner to all you love on earth—
What's that? The oil'd machinery of Love,
The cogs that twist in Venus—and after that,
Yes, after that, you feast on *"sentiment"*—
'Tis your own word—weep tender nights away
With sad, delicious memories of a kiss
When if you chose you might reap more than kissing—
You love—of course, you love (O sentimental!)
You tickle your heart with sweetmeats of emotion,
Glut on romantic thrills, enjoy rich passions,
Most luscious martyrdoms—plump, tasty sorrows—
By God, I've done with playing that touching role,
"The Girl I Left Behind Me"—here am I,
"The Girl Who Wouldn't be Left Behind", and trust me,
I'll smash those chaste affections of your soul,
You pudding of stale sentiment!

LAURENCE: O, *Catherine!*

CATHERINE: No more. I've done. Find other fools to dream of,
And I'll find other lads with lips more hot
Who'll clip me for a Month, perhaps, or less,
And leave me—and forget....

LAURENCE: O, *Catherine!*

CATHERINE: Weep, little man!

LAURENCE: O Kit of the Garden! Kit....
(*Exit Sterne. Catherine remains staring over the keyboard. After a pause, enter her mother.*)

MOTHER: He's gone—you've vexed him—O, to think he's gone
In tears and temper—you're a fool, you Slut....
You've botched it all . . . you should have heeded me.
Eh, lass, a Bodice carelessly open'd up
Can tempt a backward Gallant . . . what's the use!
He's gone, you fool . . . and here's that handsome Mirror
Fallen and broken....

THIEVES' KITCHEN

Good roaring pistol-boys, brave lads of gold,
Good roistering easy maids, blown cock-a-hoop
On floods of tavern-steam, I greet you! Drunk
With wild Canary, drowned in wines of old,
I'll swear your round, red faces dive and swim
Like clouds of fire-fish in a waxen tide,
    And these are seas of smoke we thieves behold.

Yet I've a mind I know what arms enchain
With flesh my shoulders... aye, and what warm legs
Wind quickly into mine... 'tis no pale mermaid,
No water-wench that floats in a smoky main
Betwixt the tankard and my knees... in faith,
I know thee, Joan, and by the beard of God,
    I'll prove to-night thy mortal parts again!

Leap, leap, fair vagabonds, your lives are short...
Dance firelit in your cauldron-fumes, O thieves,
Ram full your bellies with spiced food, gulp deep
Those goblets of thick ale—yea, feast and sport,
Ye Cyprian maids—lie with great, drunken rogues,
Jump by the fire—soon, soon your flesh must crawl
    And Tyburn flap with birds, long-necked and swart!

STARS

"These are the floating berries of the night,
   They drop their harvest in dark alleys down,
   Softly far down on groves of Venus, or on a little town
Forgotten at the world's edge—and O, their light
Unlocks all closed things, eyes and mouths, and drifts
   Quietly over kisses in a golden rain,
Drowning their flight, till suddenly the Cyprian lifts
   Her small, white face to the moon, then hides again.

"They are the warm candles of beauty, hung in blessing on high,
   Poised like bright comrades on boughs of night above:
They are the link-boys of Queen Venus, running out of the sky,
   Spilling their friendly radiance on all her ways of love.

"Should the girl's eyes be lit with swimming fire,
   O do not kiss it away, it is a star, a star!"
So cried the passionate poet to his great, romantic guitar.

But I was beating off the stars, gazing, not rhyming.
   I saw the bottomless, black cups of space
Between their clusters, and the planets climbing
   Dizzily in sick airs, and desired to hide my face.
But I could not escape those tunnels of nothingness,
   The cracks in the spinning Cross, nor hold my brain
From rushing for ever down that terrible lane,
   Infinity's trap-door, eternal and merciless.

THE GHOST

"Bees of old Spanish wine
Pipe at this Inn to-night,
Music and candleshine
   Fill the dim chambers....

"Fans toss and ladies pace,
Flutes of cold metal blow,
Maidens like winds of lace
   Tease the dark passages....

"Run, you fat kitchen-boys,
Pasties in pyramids
Rise while your masters poise
   Flagons with silver lids....

"Ha! Let the platters fume,
Jars wink and bottles drip,
Staining with smoke and spume
   Lips, tables, tapestries....

"Wenches with tousled silk,
Mouths warm and bubble eyes,
Tumble those beds of milk
   Under carved canopies....

"Now let your lovers dive
Deep to that hurricane....
O, to be there alive,
   Breathing again!"

So the ghost cried, and pressed to the dark pane,
Like a white leaf, his face... in vain... in vain..

UNDINE

In Undine's mirror the cutpurse found
Five candlesticks by magic drowned,
Like boughs of silver . . . and pale as death,
Biting his beard, till the rogue's own breath
Shook all their gourds of fire, he stopped,
Eyed the gilt baskets, gaped half-round. . . .
  Then down to the floor his pistol dropped. . . .

No sound in the dark rooms . . . the clank
Of metal and beam died fast . . . and flank
Pressed in strange fear to Undine's bed,
The robber stared long, and bent his head
To that soft wave . . . then hand on silk,
Plumbed the warm valley where nightly sank
  Undine the water-maid, caved in milk.

And over those pools, the rogue could smell
Rich essences globed and stoppered well
On Undine's table . . . and row by row,
Jars of green china foamed stiff with snow,
And crystal trays and bottles of stone
Bowed like black slaves to that ivory shell,
  The body of Undine . . . but Undine was gone.

Only below the candles' gleam,
In one small casket of waxen cream
With sidelong eyes the thief could follow
That rosy trough, the printed hollow
Of Undine's finger . . . then out to the street
He sprawled and fled . . . but still on the beam
  His pistol waited for Undine's feet!

NEXT TURN

No pause! The buried pipes ring out,
    The flour-faced Antic runs from sight;
Now Columbine, with scarlet pout,
    Floats in the smoking moon of light.

Now programmes wave, heads bend between—
    The roaring Years go past in file.
Soon there's the Transformation Scene—
    And then the Footmen down the aisle.

For you must wait, before you leave
    This Theatre of Varieties,
Their frozen fingers on your sleeve,
    Their most respectful "Now, sir, please!"

Out in the night, the Carriage stands,
    Plumed with black trees. The Post-boys grin.
The Coachman beats upon his hands.
    Turn after Turn goes on within.

CITY NIGHTFALL

Smoke upon smoke; over the stone lips
Of chimneys bleeding, a darker fume descends.
Night, the old nun, in voiceless pity bends
   To kiss corruption, so fabulous her pity.

All drowns in night. Even the lazar drowns
In earth at last, and rises up afresh,
Married to dust with an Infanta's flesh—
   So night, like earth, receives this poisoned city,

Charging its air with beauty, coasting its lanterns
With mains of darkness, till the leprous clay
Dissolves, and pavements drift away,
   And there is only the quiet noise of planets feeding.

And those who chafe here, limed on the iron twigs,
No greater seem than sparrows, all their cries,
Their clockwork and their merchandise,
   Frolic of painted dolls. I pass unheeding.

ADVENTURE BAY

S̲o̲p̲h̲i̲e̲'s my world ... my arm must soon or later
Like Francis Drake turn circumnavigator,
Stem the dark tides, take by the throat strange gales
And toss their spume to stars unknown, as kings
Rain diamonds to the mob ... then arch my sails
By waterspouts of lace and bubbling rings
Gulfed in deep satin, conquer those warmer waves
Where none but mermaids ride, and the still caves
Untrod by sailors ... aye, and with needle set,
Rounding Cape Turnagain, take up my way,
And so to the Ivory Coast ... and farther yet,
   Port of all drownéd lovers, Adventure Bay!

THE NIGHT-RIDE

Gas flaring on the yellow platform; voices running up and
    down;
Milk-tins in cold dented silver; half-awake I stare,
Pull up the blind, blink out—all sounds are drugged;
The slow blowing of passengers asleep;
Engines yawning; water in heavy drips;
Black, sinister travellers, lumbering up the station,
One moment in the window, hooked over bags;
Hurrying, unknown faces—boxes with strange labels—
All groping clumsily to mysterious ends,
Out of the gaslight, dragged by private Fates.
Their echoes die. The dark train shakes and plunges;
Bells cry out; the night-ride starts again.
Soon I shall look out into nothing but blackness,
Pale, windy fields. The old roar and knock of the rails
Melts in dull fury. Pull down the blind. Sleep. Sleep.
Nothing but grey, rushing rivers of bush outside.
Gaslight and milk-cans. Of Rapptown I recall nothing else.

A SUNSET

The old Quarry, Sun, with bleeding scales,
    Flaps up the gullies, wets their crystal pebbles,
Floating with waters of gold; darkness exhales
    Brutishly in the valley; smoke rises in bubbles;
Suddenly we stop at the meeting of two trails.
"Do you remember?"
        "But now everything is changed—
Trees ringed with death, the creek with its bells clanking
    Dried like white bone." Even our voices are estranged.
Darkness chokes the river; so nearly what I am thinking
    It echoes, the whole thing might have been arranged!

REALITIES

(To the etchings of Norman Lindsay)

Now the statues lean over each to each, and sing,
Gravely in warm plaster turning; the hedges are dark.
The trees come suddenly to flower with moonlight,
The water-gardens to glassy fire, and the night, the night,
Breaks in a rain of stars. O, now the statues wake,
Poise on their leaden stems, and dive into the lake—
And the old Gardener, who has grown old with raking,
   Bends by his flickering candle, and hears the noise,
And is nodding his head at a music of copper shaking,
   And Mercury whispering to some little graven Boys.

And Venus with Venus is walking in a misty grove,
Their mouths breathless with great lies of Jove,
And the green-silver moon flows quivering down their sides,
Till each is lined in light.
"And this Brass Tower?" she said—
But a stone Faun, clawed to the branches overhead,
Could hold his breath no longer, downward slides,
And crashes in a storm of leaves.—O, look, the lake!
   O, the great dolphins from the fountain-rim,
And the rusty Tritons—and O, the branches break—
   A flute of ivory shines—it is Apollo come to swim!

Then the skies open with a light from no moon or star,
The dark terraces tremble, melt in a shower of petals;
Flowers turn to faces; faces, like small gold panes,
Are bodied with a mist of limbs—no dark remains,
Nor silence, but there is laughter like bells in air,
A rushing wind of music, torches, dancers everywhere,

And lovers no farther. It is not night nor day,
The world's tissue has utterly crumbled away,
Time is a crusty pond, and that old Mirror, Life,
Has broken, and the ghosts of flesh are stirred
    With a new blood, the fluid of eternity,
And mouths that have never spoken, ears that have never heard,
    Eyes that have never seen, speak now, and hear, and see.

And I, who have climbed in these unrooted boughs
    Behind the world, find substance there and flesh,
Thoughts more infrangible than windy vows,
Love that's more bodily, and kisses longer,
And Cythera lovelier, and the girls of moonlight stronger
    Than all earth's ladies, webbed in their bony mesh.
The statues dance, and the old Gardener is asleep,
And golden bodies tread the paths—O, happy shapes,
O, shining ones! Could I for ever keep
Within your radiance, made absolute at last,
No more amongst earth's phantoms to be cast,
No more in the shadowy race of the world exist,
But, born into reality, remember Life
    As men see ghosts at midnight—so with me
Might all those aery textures, the world's mist,
    Melt into Beauty's actuality!

MUSIC

I

Music, on the air's edge, rides alone,
    Plumed like empastured Caesars of the sky
    With a god's helmet; now, in the gold dye
Of sunlight, the iron cloak, the Tuscan stone,
Melt to enchanted flesh—a voice is blown
    Down from the windy pit, like a star falling.
    Men think it is a lost eagle calling,
But the fool and the lover know it for Music's cry.

He is running with the Valkyrs on a road of manes,
    Darkness draws back its fur, the stars course by,
Fighting the windy beaks of hurricanes
    To keep their stations in the sky—
Away, away! The little earth-light wanes,
    The moon has drowned herself, cold music rings,
The battering of a thousand Vulcanals
    Hammers the blood; a thousand horsemen fly
Belly to air, away! Now Music sings
    Harshly, like horns of Tartars blown on high.

II

A ship in hell marooned;
He lies under the mast,
Caked with the sticky unguents of the sun.
Sluggishly at his wound,
The rat Pain, biting with bloody teeth
And broken nails, is fed at last,
The tale is done.
Let the shell of bleeding flesh remain,

This crusted finery is nothing worth.
He flings his body carelessly to Pain,
Meat for the earth.
Trumpets of godhood! The voice of Music sings,
Lost in the dark forest, riding out,
Louder and nearer, with triumphant wings,
Music and his eternal cavaliers—
Now *Tristan* rises with a mighty shout.
Nobody hears.

III

O, SILENT night, dark beach,
Drowning like lovers, each in each,
Uncharge thy musky boughs, unbend
Thy mouths of air, and give them speech—

Then, like a nest of thieves,
The golden, tattling leaves
Will sell their mask for bravoes' love,
Or cry their fruit to stranger Eves,

And voices ride
By foam and field
Of drowsy lovers, lips unsealed,
Blown to the lazy tide—

"With love we put the planets out,
With kissing drowned the bells,
And struck the clambering moon to ice;
Now we shall sleep and hide . . ."
I sang with Nonie, side by side,
Sunk in a drift of tumbled laces,
Till Music breathed his enormous flute
Over our small, upturned faces.

IV

In the pans of straw-coned country
This river is the solitary traveller;
Nothing else moves, the sky lies empty,
Birds there are none, and cattle not many.
Now it is sunlight, what is the difference?
Nothing. The sun is as white as moonlight.
Wind has buffeted flat the grasses,
Long, long ago; but now there is nothing,
Wind gone and men gone, only the water
Stumbling over the stones in silence—
Nothing but fields with roots gone rotten,
Paddocks unploughed and clotted marshes.
Even the wind that stirred them has vanished,
Only the river remains with its water,
Shambling over the straw-coned country.
Nothing else moves, the sky lies empty,
Only the river remains with its water,
And droughts will come. . . .

V

In and out the countryfolk, the carriages and carnival,
Pastry-cooks in all directions push to barter their confections,
Trays of little gilded cakes, caramels in painted flakes,
Marzipan of various makes and macaroons of all complexions,
Riding on a tide of country faces.
Up and down the smoke and crying,
Girls with apple-eyes are flying,
Country boys in costly braces
Run with red, pneumatic faces;
Trumpets gleam, whistles scream,
Organs cough their coloured steam out,
Dogs are worming, sniffing, squirming;

Air-balloons and paper moons,
Roundabouts with curdled tunes,
Drowned bassoons and waggon-jacks;
Tents like flowers of candle-wax;
"Buy, buy, buy, buy!
Cotton ties, cakes and pies, what a size, test your eyes, hair-dyes,
    candy-shies, all a prize, penny tries, no lies, watch it rise,
    buy, buy, buy, buy!"
So everybody buys.

Gently the doctor of magic mutters,
Opens his puppet-stall,
Pulls back the painted shutters,
Ruffles the golden lace.
Ha! The crowd flutters...
Reddened and sharp and small,
O, *Petroushka's* face!

VI

TORCHES and running fire; the flagstones drip
Like a black mirror, wet from killing. Smoke goes up,
Clouding the gilded rafter-birds, and the flying cup
That floats with magic wine to Konchak's lip.

Then the Khan claps his beard, and harps are brushed
Clear in the darkness; dancers' bells far off
Blab at their ankles. Now, from the gold trough,
We have dipped bowls of mare's milk; all is hushed.

Suddenly, dull bubbling drums uprise, grow thicker,
Split with a scream of metal—glazed in the flare,
Tartar girls rapidly whirl in storms of animal hair,
Spinning in islands of movement, quicker and quicker.

In the middle of the dance, smiling at his whim,
Khan Konchak rose, and left the golden hall.
Soon there was silent darkness over all.
One of the dancers was sent after him.

VII

In the apple-country, in the apple-trees,
The boughs are bubbling with pink snow
To frost the fields. A thousand birds fall crying,
Sharp and sweet, like morning-stars, in seas
Deeper than air. A thousand blossoms blow,
Drops of gold blood, like flowers gone flying,
Drowning with foam the drowsy girls below.

These country-girls, in hats of straw,
Take kissing as a natural law,
Put up their cheeks, like rosy saucers,
Gravely on tiptoe waiting.
They plainly do not know the dangers
This practice breeds from courteous strangers,
Who find, on airing their politeness,
Such local customs captivating.

As for my part, under the trees,
I found a girl with tawny knees,
Pretty enough, at a hurried view.
We lay on blossoms, glassed with dew.
I didn't notice her till we kissed.
How pleasant, a sentimentalist!

VIII

Open! It is the moon knocking with fists of air
To break thy doors down, it is the lusty moon
More clamorous than hunting-cries, come tramping
With lanterns to uprouse thee, drown the fields

In drifts of crystal, waken the farms with light,
And lovers call to buffet the rough smoke
From valleys rising up—then, like the juice
Of Juno's apples, the rich, Indian glow
Shall cast them out of Time, and all be running,
Dancing and kissing, in this headlong, breathless moon,
This moon pulling at old hinges, bawling through keyholes,
Crying out "*Siegmund! Siegmund! Siegmund!*"
            The door flies open.

In this house, there is anger, in the forest, night,
But love is under my laughter, and under my cloak, flight.
O, hast thou not yet woken?
In night, there is bitterness, in sorrow, tears to weep,
But love is under my music, and under my cloak, sleep.
O, Lady, hast thou spoken?
In tears, there is remembering, in memory, no release,
But love is under my kissing, and under my cloak, peace.
O, hide beneath my cloak!

So shall we steal into the deeps of Spring,
Clasped each to each, and swim the merry tide,
Rounding the world, on the green floods astride,
Till, drowned in a bubble of flowers, too dazed to cling,
We're thrown up, pink and naked castaways,
On some old beach, where Time is put to rout,
And the world a buried star, not talked about—
So shall we daunt the gods, conceal their gaze.

IX

Once, at your words, I would have struck to flame
The ground I strode on, all the hives of blood
Gone bursting mad—but now, congealed and thick,
Anger, the wine, chokes me, hoods me with stone,
Clogs and corrodes me with its marish flood.

Suddenly, as though to metal grown,
I stand immovable, feel strangely sick,
And hear your voice far off, crying my name.

The clouds dissolve. Now I can see your face,
Immense and sweating; the room has fallen in,
Tiny beside it—your face, immense and sweating,
Blurred into mockery at the words that fill you.
Come, then. You wish to crush me. Let us begin;
Since it is obvious I shall have to kill you,
Have done with useless voices and regretting.
I want to get it over, and leave this place.

Then, like some god on a stone pedestal
Who stirs by night with unfamiliar limbs,
I turn to an automaton, upraise
Half-wondering an arm I find in the air,
Clammy with grappled iron. Everything swims,
Fogged in the coughing gas-light. Blindly I stare,
And stab once or twice . . . stabbing in a daze. . . .
No need for more. He is dead, this animal.

Dead, dead. There was no need to strike
So many times, there is no need to hide—
It's nothing to be ashamed of nowadays.
He was my enemy. Now he has perished,
Charred in the smoking ovens of my pride.
Why should the splendid fury that I cherished
Seem now to be a cold and fruitless blaze?
Good God! Can't I kill my enemy if I like!

X

NOTHING grows on the stone trees
But lanterns, frosty gourds of colour,
Melting their bloody drops in water
Over the dark seas.

These peaks of stucco, smoking light,
These Venice-roads, the pools and channels,
Tunnel the night with a thousand planets,
Daubing their glaze of white,

Where belfries glitter, spire on spire,
Shining on men with paper faces,
And boats, in the glass billow fading,
Beetles of cloudy fire.

Faintly the dripping, crystal strings
Unlock their Spanish airs, their festival
Which, far away, resolves to emptiness,
Echoes of bitter things,

Far away music, cold and small,
Which, like a child's delight remembered,
Falls to mocked effigy for ever,
Melancholy to recall.

XI

COME in your painted coaches, friends of mine,
We'll keep the stars night-company with wine,
Morning shall find us bending to the flute,
And daybreak mock us at our candleshine.

Pile all thy jewelled berries in a heap,
Almonds and musk and sweetmeats, all for thee—
We'll rest on silk a thousand cushions deep,
Wake up and shake the cassia-tree,
And eat a sticky cake, and sleep,
And slee—..

XII

Look up! Thou hast a shining Guest
   Whose body in the dews hath lain,
His face like a strange wafer pressed
   Secret and starry, at thy pane;
And he shall sing with human tongue
Old music men have never sung
Since Orpheus on earth was young,
   And shall not sing again.

But life and all its lies of stone
   Shall crack to fumes and disappear,
Thy little golden shells be blown
   Like stars in water, far and near,
And thou shalt wake behind the Glass,
In stone dissolved, and phantom brass—
O, deaf! The bells of Music pass,
   Not can, but darest, thou hear!

CAPTAIN DOBBIN

Captain Dobbin, having retired from the South Seas
In the dumb tides of 1900, with a handful of shells,
A few poisoned arrows, a cask of pearls,
And five thousand pounds in the colonial funds,
Now sails the street in a brick villa, "Laburnum Villa",
In whose blank windows the harbour hangs
Like a fog against the glass,
Golden and smoky, or stoned with a white glitter,
And boats go by, suspended in the pane,
Blue Funnel, Red Funnel, Messageries Maritimes,
Lugged down the port like sea-beasts taken alive
That scrape their bellies on sharp sands,
Of which particulars Captain Dobbin keeps
A ledger sticky with ink,
Entries of time and weather, state of the moon,
Nature of cargo and captain's name,
For some mysterious and awful purpose
Never divulged.
For at night, when the stars mock themselves with lanterns,
So late the chimes blow loud and faint
Like a hand shutting and unshutting over the bells,
Captain Dobbin, having observed from bed
The lights, like a great fiery snake, of the *Comorin*
Going to sea, will note the hour
For subsequent recording in his gazette.

But the sea is really closer to him than this,
Closer to him than a dead, lovely woman,
For he keeps bits of it, like old letters,
Salt tied up in bundles
Or pressed flat,
What you might call a lock of the sea's hair,

So Captain Dobbin keeps his dwarfed memento,
His urn-burial, a chest of mummied waves,
Gales fixed in print, and the sweet dangerous countries
Of shark and casuarina-tree,
Stolen and put in coloured maps,
Like a flask of seawater, or a bottled ship,
A schooner caught in a glass bottle;
But Captain Dobbin keeps them in books,
Crags of varnished leather
Pimply with gilt, by learned mariners
And masters of hydrostatics, or the childish tales
Of simple heroes, taken by Turks or dropsy.
So nightly he sails from shelf to shelf
Or to the quadrants, dangling with rusty screws,
Or the hanging-gardens of old charts,
So old they bear the authentic protractor-lines,
Traced in faint ink, as fine as Chinese hairs.

Over the flat and painted atlas-leaves
His reading-glass would tremble,
Over the fathoms, pricked in tiny rows,
Water shelving to the coast.
Quietly the bone-rimmed lens would float
Till, through the glass, he felt the barbèd rush
Of bubbles foaming, spied the albicores,
The blue-fined admirals, heard the wind-swallowed cries
Of planters running on the beach
Who filched their swags of yams and ambergris,
Birds' nests and sandalwood, from pastures numbed
By the sun's yellow, too meek for honest theft;
But he, less delicate robber, climbed the walls,
Broke into dozing houses
Crammed with black bottles, marish wine
Crusty and salt-corroded, fading prints,
Sparkle-daubed almanacs and playing cards,
With rusty cannon, left by the French outside,
Half-buried in sand,

Even to the castle of Queen Pomaree
In the Yankee's footsteps, and found her throne-room piled
With golden candelabras, mildewed swords,
Guitars and fowling-pieces, tossed in heaps
With greasy cakes and flung-down calabashes.

Then Captain Dobbin's eye,
That eye of wild and wispy scudding blue,
Voluptuously prying, would light up
Like mica scratched by gully-suns,
And he would be fearful to look upon
And shattering in his conversation;
Nor would he tolerate the harmless chanty,
No "*Shenandoah*", or the dainty mew
That landsmen offer in a silver dish
To Neptune, sung to pianos in candlelight.
Of these he spoke in scorn,
For there was but one way of singing "*Stormalong*",
He said, and that was not really singing,
But howling, rather—shrieked in the wind's jaws
By furious men; not tinkled in drawing-rooms
By lap-dogs in clean shirts.
And, at these words,
The galleries of photographs, men with rich beards,
Pea-jackets and brass buttons, with folded arms,
Would scowl approval, for they were shipmates, too,
Companions of no cruise by reading-glass,
But fellows of storm and honey from the past—
"The Charlotte, Java, '93,"
"Knuckle and Fred at Port au Prince,"
"William in his New Rig,"
Even that notorious scoundrel, Captain Baggs,
Who, as all knew, owed Dobbin Twenty Pounds
Lost at fair cribbage, but he never paid,
Or paid "with the slack of the tops'l sheets"
As Captain Dobbin frequently expressed it.

There were their faces, grilled a trifle now,
Cigar-hued in various spots
By the brown breath of sodium-eating years,
On quarter-decks long burnt to the water's edge,
A resurrection of the dead by chemicals.
And the voyages they had made,
Their labours in a country of water,
Were they not marked by inadequate lines
On charts tied up like skins in a rack?
Or his own Odysseys, his lonely travels,
His trading days, an autobiography
Of angles and triangles and lozenges
Ruled tack by tack across the sheet,
That with a single scratch expressed the stars,
Merak and Alamak and Alpherat,
The wind, the moon, the sun, the clambering sea,

Sails bleached with light, salt in the eyes,
Bamboos and Tahiti oranges,
From some forgotten countless day,
One foundered day from a forgotten month.
A year sucked quietly from the blood,
Dead with the rest, remembered by no more
Than a scratch on a dry chart—
Or when the return grew too choking bitter-sweet
And laburnum-berries manifestly tossed
Beyond the window, not the fabulous leaves
Of Hotoo or canoe-tree or palmetto,
There were the wanderings of other keels,
Magellan, Bougainville and Cook,
Who found no greater a memorial
Than footprints over a lithograph.

For Cook he worshipped, that captain with the sad
And fine white face, who never lost a man
Or flinched a peril; and of Bougainville
He spoke with graceful courtesy, as a rival

To whom the honours of the hunting-field
Must be accorded. Not so with the Spaniard,
Sebastian Juan del Cano, at whom he sneered
Openly, calling him a fool of fortune
Blown to a sailors' abbey by chance winds
And blindfold currents, who slept in a fine cabin,
Blundered through five degrees of latitude,
Was bullied by mutineers a hundred more,
And woke and found himself across the world.

Coldly in the window,
Like a fog rubbed up and down the glass
The harbour, bony with mist
And ropes of water, glittered; and the blind tide
That crawls it knows not where, nor for what gain,
Pushed its drowned shoulders against the wheel,
Against the wheel of the mill.
Flowers rocked far down
And white, dead bodies that were anchored there
In marshes of spent light.
Blue Funnel, Red Funnel,
The ships went over them, and bells in engine-rooms
Cried to their bowels of flaring oil,
And stokers groaned and sweated with burnt skins,
Clawed to their shovels.
But quietly in his room,
In his little cemetery of sweet essences
With fond memorial-stones and lines of grace,
Captain Dobbin went on reading about the sea.

THE ATLAS

1. THE KING OF CUCKOOZ

[*"The Platt of Argier and the Pts. adioning within the view thereof made by Robert Norton the Muster Mr. of his Ma't's Fleet ther Ao Di 1620 & by his owne carfull & dilligent observations then not without danger."*]

THE King of Cuckooz Contrey
Hangs peaked above Argier
With Janzaries and Marabutts
To bid a sailor fear—

With lantern-eyed astrologers
Who walk upon the walls
And ram with stars their basilisks
Instead of cannon-balls.

And in that floating castle
(I tell you it is so)
Five thousand naked Concubines
With dulcimers do go.

Each rosy nose anoints a tile,
Bang, bang! the fort salutes,
When He, the King of Cuckooz Land,
Comes forth in satin boots,

Each rosy darling flies before
When he desires his tent,
Or, like a tempest driving flowers,
Inspects a battlement.

And this I spied by moonlight
Behind a royal bamboo—
That Monarch in a curricle
Which ninety virgins drew;

That Monarch drinking nectar
(Lord God, my tale attest!)
Milked from a snow-white elephant
As white as *your* white breast!

And this is no vain fable
As other knaves may lie—
Have I not got that Fowl aboard
Which no man may deny?

The King's own hunting-falcon
I limed across the side
When by the Bayes of Africa
King James's Fleet did ride.

What crest is there emblazoned,
Whose mark is this, I beg,
Stamped on the silver manacle
Around that dainty leg?

Let this be news to you, my dear,
How Man should be revered;
Though I'm no King of Cuckooz Land,
Behold as fierce a beard!

I have as huge an appetite,
As deep a kiss, my girl,
And *somewhere*, for the hand that seeks,
Perhaps a Sultan's pearl!

THE ATLAS

2. Post-roads

[*"The Traveller's Guide, or A Most Exact Description of the Roads of England; being Mr. Ogilby's Actual Survey and Mensuration by the Wheel, &c."*]

Post-roads that clapped with tympan heels
Of tilburies and whiskys rapidly spanking,
Where's now the tireless ghost of *Ogilby*?
Post-roads
That buoyed the rich and plunging springs
Of coaches vaster than Escurials,
Where now does *Ogilby* propel that Wheel,
What milestones does he pause to reprimand,
In what unmapped savanna of dumb shades?

Ye know not—ye are silent—brutish ducts
Numbed by the bastinadoes of iron boots,
Three hundred years asnore. Do you forget
The phaetons and fiacres, flys and breaks,
The world of dead men staring out of glass
That drummed upon your bones? Do you forget
Those nostrils oozing smoke, those floating tails,
Those criniers whipped with air?

And kidnapped lights,
Floats of rubbed yellow towed from window-panes,
Rushing their lozenges through headlong stones;
And smells of hackneys, mohair sour with damp,
Leather and slopped madeira, partridge-pies
Long-buried under floors; and yawning Fares
With bumping flap-dark spatulas of cards—
"Knave takes the ten . . . oh, God, I wish that it,
I wish that it was Guildford". . . .

Ogilby
Did not forget, could not escape such ecstacies,
Even in the monasteries of mensuration,
Could not forget the roads that he had gone
In fog and shining air. Each line was joy,
Each computation a beatitude,
A diagram of Ogilby's eye and ear
With soundings for the nose. Wherefore I think,

Wherefore I think some English gentleman,
Some learned doctor of the steak-houses,
Ending late dinner, having strolled outside
To quell the frivolous hawthorn, may behold
There in the moonshine, rolling up an hill,
Steered by no fleshly hand, with spokes of light,
The *Wheel—John Ogilby's Wheel—*the *WHEEL*
    hiss by,
Measuring mileposts of eternity.

THE ATLAS

3. Dutch Seacoast

[*"Toonneel der Steden van vereenighde Nederlanden met hare Beschrijvingen uytgegeven by Joan. Blaeu."*]

    No wind of Life may strike within
    This little country's crystal bin,
    Nor calendar compute the days
    Tubed in their capsule of soft glaze.

    Naked and rinsed, the bubble-clear
    Canals of Amsterdam appear,
    The blue-tiled turrets, china clocks
    And glittering beaks of weathercocks.

A gulf of sweet and winking hoops
Whereon there ride 500 poops
With flying mouths and fleeting hair
Of saints hung up like candles there—

Fox-coloured mansions, lean and tall,
That burst in air but never fall
Whose bolted shadows, row by row,
Float changeless on the stones below—

Sky full of ships, bay full of town,
A port of waters jellied brown:
Such is the world no tide may stir,
Sealed by the great cartographer.

O, could he but clap up like this
My decomposed metropolis,
Those other countries of the mind,
So tousled, dark and undefined!

THE ATLAS

4. Mermaids

[*"A New and Accurat Map of the World, in two Hemispheres, Western and Eastern, with the Heavens and Elements, a Figure of the Spheare, the Eclipse of the Sunne, the Eclipse of the Moon."*—J. Speed, 1675.]

Once Mermaids mocked your ships
With wet and scarlet lips
And fish-dark difficult hips, Conquistador;
Then Ondines danced with Sirens on the shore,
Then from his cloudy stall, you heard the Kraken call,
And, mad with twisting flame, the Firedrake roar.

Such old-established Ladies
No mariner eyed askance,
But, coming on deck, would swivel his neck
To watch the darlings dance,
Or in the gulping dark of nights
Would cast his tranquil eyes
On singular kinds of Hermaphrodites
Without the least surprise.

Then portulano maps were scrolled
With compass-roses, green and gold,
That fired the stiff old Needle with their dyes
And wagged their petals over parchment skies.

Then seas were full of Dolphins' fins,
Full of swept bones and flying Jinns,
Beaches were filled with Anthropophagi
And Antient Africa with Palanquins.

Then sailors, with a flaked and rice-pale flesh
Staring from maps in sweet and poisoned places,
Diced the old Skeleton afresh
In brigs no bigger than their moon-bunched faces.

Those well-known and respected Harpies
Dance no more on the shore to and fro;
All that has ended long ago;
Nor do they sing outside the captain's porthole,
A proceeding fiercely reprehended
By the governors of the P. & O.

Nor do they tumble in the sponges of the moon
For the benefit of tourists in the First Saloon,
Nor fork their foaming lily-fins below the side
On the ranges of the ale-clear tide.

And scientists now, with binocular-eyes,
Remark in a tone of complacent surprise:
"Those pisciform mammals—pure Spectres, I fear—
Must be Doctor Gerbrandus's *Mermaids*, my dear!"

But before they can cause the philosopher trouble,
They are *GONE* like the cracking of a bubble.

THE ATLAS

5. THE SEAFIGHT

[*"Archipeague du Mexique ou sont les Isles de Cuba, Espagnole, Jamaique, &c."*—SANSON, 1962.]

HERE in a gulf of golden leaf
You'll find a seafight ringed with flame;
Cannons that cry Tirduf, Tirduf,
Daggers that collop, guns that maim;
Jaws beaked with blood, men flung to hell,
Men blasting trumpets, men that flee,
Men crimped by death, and under all
Old patient, baleful, spying Sea—

Old Sea, that in a dicebox rolls
Their trundling skulls, their jacks of bone,
That sucks them out of broken hulls
When other mumbling mouths have gone—
Old hungry Sea, that holds our flesh
In the huge forceps of the storm,
And they are given to the fish
And we plucked forth, and we made warm.

But ye that kill, why heed the face
Of Ocean? Not alone you slay,
Since deeper seas are dammed in space
And fiercer storms can scream in clay;
Existence has as bitter teeth,
But we can always find a minute
For the festivities of death
Who sail upon this dangerous planet.

TO MYSELF

AFTER all, you are my rather tedious hero;
It is impossible (damn it!) to avoid
Looking at you through keyholes.
But come! At least you might try to be
Even, let us say, a Graceful Zero
Or an Eminent Molecule, gorgeously employed.

Have you not played Hamlet's father in the wings
Long enough, listening to poets groan,
Seeking a false catharsis
In flesh not yours, through doors ajar
In the houses of dead kings,
In the gods' tombs, in the coffins of cracked stone?

Have you not poured yourself, thin fluid mind,
Down the dried-up canals, the powdering creeks,
Whose waters none remember
Either to praise them or condemn,
Whose fabulous cataracts none can find
Save one who has forgotten what he seeks?

Your uncle, the Great Harry, left after him
The memory of a cravat, a taste in cheese,
And a way of saying "I am honoured."
Such things, when men and beasts have gone,
Smell sweetly to the seraphim.
Believe me, fool, there are worse gifts than these.

ELEGY IN A BOTANIC GARDENS

The smell of birds' nests faintly burning
Is autumn. In the autumn I came
Where spring had used me better,
To the clear red pebbles and the men of stone
And foundered beetles, to the broken Meleager
And thousands of white circles drifting past,
Cold suns in water; even to the dead grove
Where we had kissed, to the Tristania tree
Where we had kissed so awkwardly,
Noted by swans with damp, accusing eyes,
All gone to-day; only the leaves remain,
Gaunt paddles ribbed with herringbones
Of watermelon-pink. Never before
Had I assented to the hateful name
Meryta Macrophylla, on a tin tag.
That was no time for botany. But now the schools,
The horticulturists, come forth
Triumphantly with Latin. So be it now,
Meryta Macrophylla, and the old house,
Ringed with black stone, no Georgian Headlong Hall
With glass-eye windows winking candles forth,
Stuffed with French horns, globes, air-pumps, telescopes
And Cupid in a wig, playing the flute,
But truly, and without escape,
THE NATIONAL HERBARIUM,
Repeated dryly in Roman capitals,
THE NATIONAL HERBARIUM.

TRADE CIRCULAR

(*To the Poets' Ladies*)

SHALL I give you the Bourbon-sugars
Of sherry and yellow sky
And a girl in a country curricle
Merrily bowling by?

Or darkness flying with crystals,
And the great Miser, Night,
Rubbing a mountain's breast-bone
With an old rind of light?

Wake up the handcuffed angels,
Muster the marble kings,
Till the blood swims in their bodies
And the stone captain sings?

Ask for a cage of comets,
Poets will give you this—
But if you should ask them for nothing,
They'll see how dead girls kiss.

FIVE VISIONS OF CAPTAIN COOK

I

Cook was a captain of the Admiralty
When sea-captains had the evil eye,
Or should have, what with beating krakens off
And casting nativities of ships;
Cook was a captain of the powder-days
When captains, you might have said, if you had been
Fixed by their glittering stare, half-down the side,
Or gaping at them up companionways,
Were more like warlocks than a humble man—
And men were humble then who gazed at them,
Poor horn-eyed sailors, bullied by devils' fists
Of wind or water, or the want of both,
Childlike and trusting, filled with eager trust—
Cook was a captain of the sailing days
When sea-captains were kings like this,
Not cold executives of company-rules
Cracking their boilers for a dividend
Or bidding their engineers go wink
At bells and telegraphs, so plates would hold
Another pound. Those captains drove their ships
By their own blood, no laws of schoolbook steam,
Till yards were sprung, and masts went overboard—
Daemons in periwigs, doling magic out,
Who read fair alphabets in stars
Where humbler men found but a mess of sparks,
Who steered their crews by mysteries
And strange, half-dreadful sortilege with books,
Used medicines that only gods could know
The sense of, but sailors drank
In simple faith. That was the captain
Cook was when he came to the Coral Sea
And chose a passage into the dark.

How many mariners had made that choice
Paused on the brink of mystery! "Choose now!"
The winds roared, blowing home, blowing home,
Over the Coral Sea. "Choose now!" the trades
Cried once to Tasman, throwing him for choice
Their teeth or shoulders, and the Dutchman chose
The wind's way, turning north. "Choose, Bougainville!"
The wind cried once, and Bougainville had heard
The voice of God, calling him prudently
Out of a dead lee shore, and chose the north.
The wind's way. So, too, Cook made choice,
Over the brink, into the devil's mouth,
With four months' food, and sailors wild with dreams
Of English beer, the smoking barns of home.
So Cook made choice, so Cook sailed westabout,
So men write poems in Australia.

II

FLOWERS turned to stone! Not all the botany
Of Joseph Banks, hung pensive in a porthole,
Could find the Latin for this loveliness,
Could put the Barrier Reef in a glass box
Tagged by the horrid Gorgon squint
Of horticulture. Stone turned to flowers
It seemed—you'd snap a crystal twig,
One petal even of the water-garden,
And have it dying like a cherry-bough.

They'd sailed all day outside a coral hedge,
And half the night. Cook sailed at night,
Let there be reefs a fathom from the keel
And empty charts. The sailors didn't ask,
Nor Joseph Banks. Who cared? It was the spell

Of Cook that lulled them, bade them turn below,
Kick off their sea-boots, puff themselves to sleep,
Though there were more shoals outside
Than teeth in a shark's head. Cook snored loudest himself.

One day, a morning of light airs and calms,
They slid towards a reef that would have knifed
Their boards to mash, and murdered every man.
So close it sucked them, one wave shook their keel.
The next blew past the coral. Three officers,
In gilt and buttons, languidly on deck
Pointed their sextants at the sun. One yawned,
One held a pencil, one put eye to lens:
Three very peaceful English mariners
Taking their sights for longitude.
I've never heard
Of sailors aching for the longitude
Of shipwrecks before or since. It was the spell
Of Cook did this, the phylacteries of Cook.
Men who ride broomsticks with a mesmerist
Mock the typhoon. So, too, it was with Cook.

III

Two chronometers the captain had,
One by Arnold that ran like mad,
One by Kendal in a walnut case,
Poor devoted creature with a hangdog face.

Arnold always hurried with a crazed click-click
Dancing over Greenwich like a lunatic,
Kendal panted faithfully his watch-dog beat,
Climbing out of Yesterday with sticky little feet.

Arnold choked with appetite to wolf up time,
Madly round the numerals his hands would climb,
His cogs rushed over and his wheels ran miles,
Dragging Captain Cook to the Sandwich Isles.

But Kendal dawdled in the tombstoned past,
With a sentimental prejudice to going fast,
And he thought very often of a haberdasher's door
And a yellow-haired boy who would knock no more.

All through the night-time, clock talked to clock,
In the captain's cabin, tock-tock-tock,
One ticked fast and one ticked slow,
And Time went over them a hundred years ago.

IV

SOMETIMES the god would fold his wings
And, stone of Caesars turned to flesh,
Talk of the most important things
That serious-minded midshipmen could wish,

Of plantains, and the lack of rum
Or spearing sea-cows—things like this
That hungry schoolboys, five days dumb,
In jolly-boats are wonted to discuss.

What midshipman would pause to mourn
The sun that beat about his ears,
Or curse the tide, if he could horn
His fists by tugging on those lumbering oars?

Let rum-tanned mariners prefer
To hug the weather-side of yards;
"Cats to catch mice" before they purr,
Those were the captain's enigmatic words.

Here, in this jolly-boat they graced,
Were food and freedom, wind and storm,
While, fowling-piece across his waist,
Cook mapped the coast, with one eye cocked for game.

V

AFTER the candles had gone out, and those
Who listened had gone out, and a last wave
Of chimney-haloes caked their smoky rings
Like fish-scales on the ceiling, a Yellow Sea
Of swimming circles, the old man,
Old Captain-in-the-Corner, drank his rum
With friendly gestures to four chairs. They stood
Empty, still warm from haunches, with rubbed nails
And leather glazed, like agèd serving-men
Feeding a king's delight, the sticky, drugged
Sweet agony of habitual anecdotes.
But these, his chairs, could bear an old man's tongue,
Sleep when he slept, be flattering when he woke,
And wink to hear the same eternal name
From lips new-dipped in rum.

"Then Captain Cook,
I heard him, told them they could go
If so they chose, but he would get them back,
Dead or alive, he'd have them,"
The old man screeched, half-thinking to hear "Cook!
Cook again! Cook! It's other cooks he'll need,
Cooks who can bake a dinner out of pence,
That's what he lives on, talks on, half-a-crown
A day, and sits there full of Cook.
Who'd do your cooking now, I'd like to ask,
If someone didn't grind her bones away?
But that's the truth, six children and half-a-crown
A day, and a man gone daft with Cook."

That was his wife,
Elizabeth, a noble wife but brisk,
Who lived in a present full of kitchen-fumes
And had no past. He had not seen her
For seven years, being blind, and that of course
Was why he'd had to strike a deal with chairs,
Not knowing when those who chafed them had gone to sleep
Or stolen away. Darkness and empty chairs,
This was the port that Alexander Home
Had come to with his useless cutlass-wounds
And tales of Cook, and half-a-crown a day—
This was the creek he'd run his timbers to,
Where grateful countrymen repaid his wounds
At half-a-crown a day. Too good, too good,
This eloquent offering of birdcages
To gulls, and Greenwich Hospital to Cook,
Britannia's mission to the sea-fowl.

It was not blindness picked his flesh away,
Nor want of sight made penny-blank the eyes
Of Captian Home, but that he lived like this
In one place, and gazed elsewhere. His body moved
In Scotland, but his eyes were dazzle-full
Of skies and water farther round the world—
Air soaked with blue, so thick it dripped like snow
On spice-tree boughs, and water diamond-green,
Beaches wind-glittering with crumbs of gilt,
And birds more scarlet than a duchy's seal
That had come whistling long ago, and far
Away. His body had gone back,
Here it sat drinking rum in Berwickshire,
But not his eyes—they were left floating there
Half-round the earth, blinking at beaches milked
By suck-mouth tides, foaming with ropes of bubbles
And huge half-moons of surf. Thus it had been
When Cook was carried on a sailor's back,
Vengeance in a cocked hat, to claim his price,

A prince in barter for a longboat.
And then the trumpery springs of fate—a stone,
A musket-shot, a round of gunpowder,
And puzzled animals, killing they knew not what
Or why, but killing . . . the surge of goatish flanks
Armoured in feathers, like cruel birds:
Wild, childish faces, killing; a moment seen,
Marines with crimson coats and puffs of smoke
Toppling face-down; and a knife of English iron,
Forged aboard ship, that had been changed for pigs,
Given back to Cook between the shoulder-blades.
There he had dropped, and the old floundering sea,
The old, fumbling, witless lover-enemy,
Had taken his breath, last office of salt water.

Cook died. The body of Alexander Home
Flowed round the world and back again, with eyes
Marooned already, and came to English coasts,
The vague ancestral darkness of home,
Seeing them faintly through a glass of gold,
Dim fog-shapes, ghosted like the ribs of trees
Against his blazing waters and blue air.
But soon they faded, and there was nothing left,
Only the sugar-cane and the wild granaries
Of sand, and palm-trees and the flying blood
Of cardinal-birds; and putting out one hand
Tremulously in the direction of the beach,
He felt a chair in Scotland. And sat down.

WILD GRAPES

The old orchard, full of smoking air,
Full of sour marsh and broken boughs, is there,
But kept no more by vanished Mulligans,
Or Hartigans, long drowned in earth themselves,
Who gave this bitter fruit their care.

Here's where the cherries grew that birds forgot,
And apples bright as dogstars; now there is not
An apple or a cherry; only grapes,
But wild ones, Isabella grapes they're called,
Small, pointed, black, like boughs of musket-shot.

Eating their flesh, half-savage with black fur.
Acid and gipsy-sweet, I thought of her,
Isabella, the dead girl, who has lingered on
Defiantly when all have gone away,
In an old orchard where swallows never stir.

Isabella grapes, outlaws of a strange bough,
That in their harsh sweetness remind me somehow
Of dark hair swinging and silver pins,
A girl half-fierce, half-melting, as these grapes,
Kissed here—or killed here—but who remembers now?

LA DAME DU PALAIS DE LA REINE

SOPHIE, in shocks of scarlet lace,
Receives her usual embrace
Beneath a hedge, behind a curtain,
Or in the chambers of His Grace.
Whether a kiss be worth the care
Five minions wasted on her hair,
Sophie herself is half uncertain,
Paused in adorable despair.

When past beseeching Man she floats
In golden-coasted petticoats,
A shaft of irritation passes;
Like colic; but with antidotes.
Then serious doubts occur of Love
That spoils the Peacock, sours the Dove,
And mixes up the lower classes
So hopelessly with those above.

Is the bird Passion worth the lime?
Can the small Amor turn to crime
By ruining skirts—and the digestion?
Such problems occupy her time.
But often these objections thaw
To counts with viols—or grooms with straw—
And Sophie, giving up the question,
Bends to some strange but natural law.

With books of music, diamond rings,
Spaniels and roses, fireworks, swings,
Her lovers come. But Sophie sighs,
Whose thoughts are fixed on Higher Things.

Between the sleepy kisses given,
Her mind by grave debate is driven,
Perplexity distracts those eyes
Which, lovers vow, are lost in Heaven!

WATERS

This Water, like a sky that no one uses,
Air turned to stone, ridden by stars and birds
No longer, but with clouds of crystal swimming,
I'll not forget, nor men can lose, though words
Dissolve with music, gradually dimming.
So let them die; whatever the mind loses,
Water remains, cables and bells remain,
Night comes, the sailors burn their riding-lamps,
And strangers, pitching on our graves their camps,
Will break through branches to the surf again.

Darkness comes down. The Harbour shakes its mane,
Glazed with a leaf of amber; lights appear
Like thieves too early, dropping their swag by night,
Red, gold and green, down trap-doors glassy-clear,
And lanterns over Pinchgut float with light
Where they so long have lain.
All this will last, but I who gaze must go
On water stranger and less clear, and melt
With flesh away; and stars that I have felt,
And loved, shall shine for eyes I do not know.

GLUBBDUBDRIB

[... *"and we all three entered the gate of the palace between two rows of guards, armed and dressed after a very antique manner, and something in the countenances that made my flesh creep with a horror I cannot express."*
—A Voyage to Laputa.]

In the castle of Glubbdubdrib
How spendidly we dine
On flesh from magic potagers
And cups of dead men's wine,

Dead men who run with bottles,
Lackeys of silent air,
A ghost in gilded livery
Fawning behind each chair.

Beckon, and flunkey Caesars
Bring us their phantom bread.
Once they were gods and emperors;
Now, of course, they are dead.

The governor of Glubbdubdrib
(Two ghosts cringe on each side)
Bows to congratulations,
Filled with a careless pride.

"Really, the servant problem....
You mean that Roman youth?
Catullus. Oh, yes, brisk enough,
But—you know—so uncouth.

"There's Plato in the passage,
They tell me he's quite droll.
He says some devilish clever things;
A heathen, though, poor soul. . . ."

The governor of Glubbdubdrib
Resumes his drinking-cup.
As for the guests and visitors,
They hadn't even looked up.

RUBENS' HELL

Venus with rosy-cloven rump
And rings of straw-bright flying hair
Looks in the glass that slaves are plying
Not for her own face floating there,
But for the sly and curious gaze
Of Rubens, through the keyhole prying.

Warm flesh of gods, by light embayed,
And drifting daemon-bones within
That sweep like music up and down
To pouts and cups of ivory skin,
Firm-valleyed croup, and swagging arm
In whose embankment bracelets drown—

Do you remain, you strokes of paint,
With Venus mocked and Rubens dead
And Beauty sold for an antique
And microscopes raised up instead?
Still are your old adherents true;
Rubens is there, if he could speak.

Rubens is there in your high room,
Rubens it is who blows his breath
To fix you laughing in the glass,
Who keeps a castle here from death
While schools go out and fashions fall
And microscopes and movements pass.

This castle-keep of joys conceived
But never sucked is Rubens' hell,
Is Rubens' limbo, cut and won

From darkness. Here he comes to dwell.
Man's heaven is the place he builds
By thoughts imagined and things done.

Some choose a paradise of gas,
And some, by pious deeds below,
The heavenly butter-hatch for flunkeys;
Who dream of nought to nothing go.
Therefore I'd sooner Rubens' hell
Than go to heaven with the donkeys.

BURYING FRIENDS

[... *"for a little of our vital essence goes into the grave of a friend."*—*"The Succubus"*, N. LINDSAY.]

BURYING friends is not a pomp,
Not, indeed, Roman:
Lacking the monument,
Heroic stone;
Nor is it an obscuring parasol,
The pad of customary gloves and cries
And a black leather mourning-carriage
Hung between death and the beholder's eyes.

This little bin of cancelled flesh
Strode the earth once,
Rubbed against men—
But that's all done.
A gentle elegy, a tear or two,
May charm the grave-diggers, no doubt,
But nothing can count to these incongrous ruins.
Their commercial value is not worth speaking about.

Only it seems not a burial
Of irrelevant sods,
But a lopped member
From this my body;
Almost, in fact, a tiny amputation,
A paring of biography, thrown in there.
And he has thieved his own life away
And something from mine. Farewell, thou pilferer!

CROW COUNTRY

GUTTED of station, noise alone,
The crow's voice trembles down the sky
As if this nitrous flange of stone
Wept suddenly with such a cry;
As if the rock found lips to sigh,
The riven earth a mouth to moan;
But we that hear them, stumbling by,
Confuse their torments with our own.

Over the huge abraded rind,
Crow-countries graped with dung, we go,
Past gullies that no longer flow
And wells that nobody can find,
Lashed by the screaming of the crow,
Stabbed by the needles of the mind.

SERENADE

THOU moon, like a white Christus hanging
At the sky's cross-roads, I'll court thee not,
Though travellers bend up, and seek thy grace.
Let them go truckle with their gifts and singing,
I'll ask no favours of thy cocker face.

Moonlight's a viand sucked by the world's lovers,
Captains and peasants, all that are young and have luck.
They take the moon. Nobody asked them to.
Let the musicians lout to thee for favours;
Personally, I have other things to do.

TALBINGO

"Talbingo River"—as one says of bones:
"Captain" or "Commodore" that smelt gunpowder
In old engagements no one quite believes
Or understands. Talbingo had its blood
As they did, ran with waters huge and clear
Lopping down mountains,
Turning crags to banks.

Now it's a sort of aching valley,
Basalt shaggy with scales,
A funnel of tobacco-coloured clay,
Smoulders of puffed earth
And pebbles and shell-bodied flies
And water thickening to stone in pocks.

That's what we're like out here,
Beds of dried-up passions.

COUNTRY TOWNS

Country towns, with your willows and squares,
And farmers bouncing on barrel mares
To public-houses of yellow wood
With "1860" over their doors,
And that mysterious race of Hogans
Which always keeps General Stores....

At the School of Arts, a broadsheet lies
Sprayed with the sarcasm of flies:
"The Great Golightly Family
Of Entertainers Here To-night"—
Dated a year and a half ago,
But left there, less from carelessness
Than from a wish to seem polite.

Verandas baked with musky sleep,
Mulberry faces dozing deep,
And dogs that lick the sunlight up
Like paste of gold—or, roused in vain
By far, mysterious buggy-wheels,
Lower their ears, and drowse again....

Country towns with your schooner bees,
And locusts burnt in the pepper-trees,
Drown me with syrups, arch your boughs,
Find me a bench, and let me snore,
Till, charged with ale and unconcern,
I'll think it's noon at half-past four!

A BUSHRANGER

JACKEY JACKEY gallops on a horse like a swallow
Where the carbines bark and the blackboys hollo.
When the traps give chase (may the Devil take his power!)
He can ride ten miles in a quarter of an hour.

Take a horse and follow, and you'll hurt no feelings;
He can fly down waterfalls and jump through ceilings,
He can shoot off hats, for to have a bit of fun,
With a bulldog bigger than a buffalo-gun.

Honeyed and profound is his conversation
When he bails up Mails on Long Tom Station,
In a flyaway coat with a black cravat,
A snow-white collar and a cabbage-tree hat.

Flowers in his button-hole and pearls in his pocket,
He comes like a ghost and he goes like a rocket
With a lightfoot heel on a blood-mare's flank
And a bagful of notes from the Joint Stock Bank.

Many pretty ladies he could witch out of marriage,
Though he prig but a kiss in a bigwig's carriage;
For the cock of an eye or the lift of his reins,
They would run barefoot through Patrick's Plains.

GULLIVER

I'LL kick your walls to bits, I'll die scratching a tunnel,
If you'll give me a wall, if you'll give me a simple stone,
If you'll do me the honour of a dungeon—
Anything but this tyranny of sinews.
Lashed with a hundred ropes of nerve and bone
I lie, poor helpless Gulliver,
In a twopenny dock for the want of a penny,
Tied up with stuff too cheap, and strings too many.
One chain is usually sufficient for a cur.

Hair over hair, I pick my cables loose,
But still the ridiculous manacles confine me.
I snap them, swollen with sobbing. What's the use?
One hair I break, ten thousand hairs entwine me.
Love, hunger, drunkenness, neuralgia, debt,
Cold weather, hot weather, sleep and age—
If I could only unloose their spongy fingers,
I'd have a chance yet, slip through the cage.
But who ever heard of a cage of hairs?
You can't scrape tunnels in a net.

If you'd give me a chain, if you'd give me honest iron,
If you'd graciously give me a turnkey,
I could break my teeth on a chain, I could bite through metal,
But what can you do with hairs?
For God's sake, call the hangman.

FIXED IDEAS

RANKS of electroplated cubes, dwindling to glitters,
Like the other pasture, the trigonometry of marble,
Death's candy-bed. Stone caked on stone,
Dry pyramids and racks of iron balls.
Life is observed, a precipitate of pellets,
Or grammarians freeze it into spar,
Their rhomboids, as for instance, the finest crystal
Fixing a snowfall under glass. Gods are laid out
In alabaster, with horny cartilage
And zinc ribs; or systems of ecstasy
Baked into bricks. There is a gallery of sculpture,
Bleached bones of heroes, Gorgon masks of bushrangers;
But the quarries are of more use than this,
Filled with the rolling of huge granite dice,
Ideas and judgments: vivisection, the Baptist Church,
Good men and bad men, polygamy, birth-control....

Frail tinkling rush
Water-hair streaming
Prickles and glitters
Cloudy with bristles
River of thought
Swimming the pebbles—
Undo, loosen your bubbles!

THE COUNTRY RIDE

[... *"Of all the Journeys that ever I made, this was the merriest, and I was in a strange mood for mirth."*—SAMUEL PEPYS, 11 April, 1661.]

EARTH which has known so many passages
Of April air, so many marriages
Of strange and lovely atoms breeding light,
Never may find again that lost delight.

In the sharp sky, the frosty deepnesses,
There are still birds to barb the silences,
There are still fields to meet the morning on,
But those who made them beautiful have gone.

Diamonds are flung by other smoking springs,
But where is he that cropped their offerings—
The pick-purse of enchantments, riding by,
Whistling his "*Go and Be Hanged, That's Twice Goodbye*"?

Who such a frolic pomp of blessing made
To kiss a little pretty dairymaid....
And country wives with bare and earth-burnt knees,
And boys with beer, and smiles from balconies....

The greensleeve girl, apprentice-equerry,
Tending great men with slant-eye mockery:
"Then Mr Sam says, 'Riding's hot,' he says,
Tasting their ale and waving twopences...."

Into one gaze they swam, a moment swirled,
One fiery paintbox of the body's world—
Into Sam's eye, that flying bushranger—
Swinging their torches for earth's voyager.

And how the blood sang, and the senses leapt,
And cells that under tents of horn had slept
Rose dancing, at the black and faceless bale
Of gallows-flesh that had not girl nor ale!

THE NABOB

(To the memory of William Hickey, Esq.)

COMING out of India with ten thousand a year
Exchanged for flesh and temper, a dry Faust
Whose devil barters with digestion, has he paid dear
For dipping his fingers in the Roc's valley?

Who knows? It's certain that he owns a rage,
A face like shark-skin, full of Yellow Jack,
And that unreckoning tyranny of age
That calls for turtles' eggs in Twickenham.

Sometimes, by moonlight, in a barge he'll float
Whilst hirelings blow their skulking flageolets,
Served by a Rajah in a golden coat
With pigeon-pie ... Madeira ... and Madeira ...

Or in his Bon de Paris with silver frogs
He rolls puff-bellied in an equipage,
Elegant chariot, through a gulf of fogs
To dine on dolphin-steak with Post-Captains.

Who knows? There are worse things than steak, perhaps,
Worse things than oyster-sauces and tureens
And worlds of provender like painted maps
Pricked out with ports of claret and pitchcocked eels,

And hubbubs of billiard-matches, burnt champagne,
Beautiful ladies "of the establishment"
Always in tempers, or melting out again,
Bailiffs and Burgundy and writs of judgment—

Thus to inhabit huge, lugubrious halls
Damp with the steam of entrees, glazed with smoke,
Raw drinking, greasy eating, bussing and brawls,
Drinking and eating and bursting into bed-chambers.

But, in the end, one says farewell to them;
And if he'd curse to-day—God damn your blood!—
Even his curses I'd not altogether condemn,
Not altogether scorn; and if phantoms ate—

Hickey, I'd say, sit down, pull up, set to:
Here's knife and fork, there's wine, and there's a barmaid.
Let us submerge ourselves in onion-soup,
Anything but this "damned profession of writing".

TOILET OF A DANDY

TRANSPORTS of filed nerves; a wistful cough;
One sensual hairbrush reluctantly concludes
The Great Harry's excruciations and beatitudes,
Delicately and gravely putting things on and off.

Shouting through shirts, dipping out liquid flowers,
All the accoutrements and mysteries,
The awful engines of the toilet—presses, trees,
And huge voluptuous bootjacks, for two shuddering hours.

But in the glass navel of his dressing-room,
Nests of diminishing mirrors, Narcissus peers,
Too nicely shined, parting the cracked, refracted sneers,
And meets the Corpse in Evening Dress; Caruso's tomb.

METEMPSYCHOSIS

SUDDENLY to become John Benbow, walking down William Street
With a tin trunk and a five-pound note, looking for a place to eat,
And a peajacket the colour of a shark's behind
That a Jew might buy in the morning....

To fry potatoes (God save us!) if you feel inclined,
Or to kiss the landlady's daughter, and no one mind,
In a peel-papered bedroom with a whistling jet
And a picture of the Holy Virgin....

Wake in a shaggy bale of blankets with a fished-up cigarette,
Picking over the "Turfbird's Tattle" for a Saturday morning bet,
With a bottle in the wardrobe easy to reach
And a blast of onions from the landing....

Tattooed with foreign ladies' tokens, a heart and dagger each,
In places that make the delicate female inquirer screech,
And over a chest smoky with gunpowder-blue—
Behold!—a mermaid piping through a coach-horn!

Banjo-playing, firing off guns, and other momentous things to do,
Such as blowing through peashooters at hawkers to improve the view—

Suddenly paid-off and forgotten in Woolloomooloo....

Suddenly to become John Benbow....

MEPHISTOPHELES PERVERTED

(Or Goethe for the Times)

ONCE long ago lived a Flea
Who kept such a fine, fat King,
Not that he held with royalty,
But more for the appearance of the thing,

And gave his Majesty to hold
(Such pageantries are far too few)
A sword of ruby-hilted gold
That possibly might hack a cheese in two;

But lest this glory might begin
To prove the regency too far,
His thunderbolt they made of tin,
And changed his godship for another Star.

Thus when the Monarch drove abroad,
With stars like buttons round his chest,
God-fearing Fleas would all applaud,
And alien Lice be grudgingly impressed.

Such relics every Flea must flaunt,
If only as the final trump
That mocks Materialism's taunt,
Proving there's more in life than Suck and Jump.

Once long ago—but not so long—
A King went curing scrofula . . .
The chorus of this charming song,
I'm told reliably, is Ha, Ha, Ha.

THE OLD PLAY

[... "*Madame, connaissez-vous cette vieille pièce? C'est une pièce tout à fait distinguée, seulement un peu trop mélancolique.*"—H. HEINE, Tambour Legrand.]

I

In an old play-house, in an old play,
In an old piece that has been done to death,
We dance, kind ladies, noble friends.
Observe our modishness, I pray,
What dignity the music lends.
Our sighs, no doubt, are only a doll's breath,
But gravely done—indeed, we're all devotion,
All pride and fury and pitiful elegance.
The importance of these antics, who may doubt?
Do you deny us the honour of emotion
Because another has danced this, our dance?
Let us jump it out.

II

In the old play-house, in the watery flare
Of gilt and candlesticks, in a dim pit
Furred with a powder of corroded plush,
Paint fallen from angels floating in mid-air,
The gods in languor sit.
Their talk they hush,
Their eyes' bright stony suction
Freezes to silence as we come
With our proud masks to act.
Who knows? Our poor induction
May take the ear, may still, perchance, distract.

Unspeakable tedium!
Is there nothing new in this old theatre, nothing new?
Are there no bristles left to prick
With monstrous tunes the music-box of flesh?
Hopes dies away; the dance, absurd, antique,
Fatigues their monocles; the gods pursue
Their ageless colloquy afresh.

III

MARDUK his jewelled finger flips
To greet a friend. Bald-headed, lean,
He wets his red transparent lips,
Taps his pince-nez, and gapes unseen.

Hequet to Mama Cocha cranes
Her horny beak. "These fools who drink
Hemlock with love deserve their pains.
They're so conventional, I think."

Limply she ceases to employ
Her little ivory spying-lens.
"I much prefer the Egyptian boy
Who poisoned Thua in the fens."

IV

BUT who are we to sneer,
Who are we to count the rhymes
Or the authorized postures of the heart
Filched from a dynasty of mimes?
Each has a part;

We do not hear
The mockers at our little, minion ardours,
Our darling hatreds and adulteries,
Our griefs and ecstasies,
Our festivals and murders.

And who are we, who are we,
That would despise the lawful ceremonies
Condoned by the coming of five Christs,
By the beating of an infinitude of breasts,
By Adam's tears, by the dead man's pennies,
Who are we?

V

AND who are we to argue with our lutes,
How would we change the play?
Are we Lucifers with hell in our boots?
There are no Lucifers to-day.
By no means. It is never like this,
Never like this. One does not fall.
How should we find, like Lucifer, an abyss?
Never like that at all.

And who are we to pester Azrael,
Importunate for funeral plumes
And all the graces Death can sell—
Death in cocked feathers, Death in drawing-rooms,
Death with a sword-cane, stabbing down the stairs?
It is not like this at all,
Never, never like this.
Death is the humblest of affairs,
It is really incredibly small:
The dropping of a degree or less,
And tightening of a vein, such gradual things.
And then
How should we guess
The slow Capuan poison, the soft strings,
Of Death with leather jaws come tasting men?

VI

CAMAZOTZ and Anubis
Go no more to the *coulisses*.
Once they'd wait for hours,
Grateful for a few excuses,
Hiding their snouts in flowers,
Merely as a tribute to the Muses.

Those were the days of serenades.
Prima donnas and appointments.
Now they think longer of pomades,
Less of the heart and more of ointments.

Anubis dabbles with the world;
A charming man, perhaps a trifle sinister,
But with his stars on, and his tendrils curled,
Really, you'd take him for the Persian Minister.

But Camazotz has grown jaded
And likes an arm-chair in the stalls,
Being by brute necessity persuaded
That perfect love inevitably palls;

Such the divine adversity
Of passion twisting on its stem,
Seeking a vague and cloudier trophy
Beyond the usual diadem.

"More balconies! More lilac-trees!
Let us go out to the private bar.
I am so tired of young men like these,
Besides, I note he is carrying a guitar."

VII

"SHANG YA! I want to be your friend"—
That was the fashion in our termitary,
In the gas-lit cellules of virtuous young men—
"Shang Ya! I want to be your friend."
Often I think, if we had gone then
Waving the torches of demoniac theory,
We should have melted stone, astonished God,
Overturned kings, exalted scullions,
And ridden the hairy beast outside
Into our stables to be shod—
Such was the infection of our pride,
Almost a confederation of Napoleons.

    Though in Yuëh it is usual
        To behead a cock and dog,
    Such was not considered binding
        In our bloodless decalogue.

    But the tail-piece to the chapter
        We so fierily began
    Resembled an old song-book
        From the golden days of Han.

Ours was the Life-Parting
Which made the poets so elegantly tragic.
On and on, always on and on,
By fears and families, by a sudden plague of logic,
By an agreeable ossification,
By a thousand tiny particles of space
Widening the fissures of our brotherhood,
We were impelled from place to place,
Dismembered by necessitude.

Who could have called that soft, adhesive nag
We bounced our lives on, a wild horse?
We were given palfreys in the place of stallions;

As for the kings and scullions,
We should, no doubt, have brought them to our flag
Had we not forgotten the prescribed discourse.

On and on, driven by flabby whips,
To the Nine Lands, to the world's end,
We have been scattered by the sea-captains of ships,
Crying no more, with bright and childish lips,
Even if we wanted to pretend,
"Shang Ya! Let me be your friend."

VIII

This is really a Complete Life and Works,
The memorial of a great man
Who was born with Excalibur in his fist
And finished by asking questions.

Woken by a star falling on his tiles,
He rushed out, defying devils—
"Come forth, you monster!" Only neighbours peeped
Fish-eyed at this ferocity.

Repeatedly inviting the rogue to stand,
He hunted with a naked sword,
But though general admiration and sympathy were expressed,
The scoundrel was not detected.

At last, regrettable to state, he stopped.
Why honour a coward with pursuit?
So he began to use Excalibur in the kitchen,
Or on occasion as a hay-rake.

How did he know that Time at length would gnaw
The rascal's face with quicklime?
Gradually the print faded, a fog blew down,
He even forgot the nature of the outrage.

However, he managed to live very tolerably,
And now, in a substantial villa,
Having saved enough to purchase an annuity,
Is piously glad he never found anyone.

But Gutumdug and Vukub-Cakix,
Having already seen many great men,
May surely be pardoned if with foundered chins
They doze a little....

Phew ... heu....
Doze a little.

IX

A BIRD sang in the jaws of night,
Like a star lost in space—
O, dauntless molecule to smite
With joy that giant face!

I heard you mock the lonely air,
The bitter dark, with song,
Waking again the old Despair
That had been dead so long,

That had been covered up with clay
And never talked about,
So none with bony claws could say
They'd dig my coffin out.

But you, with music clear and brave,
Have shamed the buried thing;
It rises dripping from the grave
And tries in vain to sing.

O, could the bleeding mouth reply,
The broken flesh but moan,
The tongues of skeletons would cry,
And Death push back his stone!

X

My strings I break, my breast I beat,
The immemorial tears repeat,
But Beli, yawning in the pit,
Is not at all impressed by it.

Fresh lachrymations to endure!
He champs a gilded comfiture—
"The song was stale five Acts ago;
Besides, it isn't Life, you know."

XI

But Life we know, but Life we know,
Is full of visions and vertigo,
Full of God's blowpipes belching rubies forth,
And God's ambiguous grape-shot maiming saints,
Full of emancipations and restraints—
Thou poor, bewildered earth!

Thou givest us neither doom nor expiation,
Nor palm-trees bursting into praise;
Blow down thy fruit, we snatch our stomachful,
Thou turnest not thy gaze,
Knowing we do but rob a little time;
A flight of air; thou takest back the spoils.
O, for some thunder on our brother's crime,
Even a little harmless flagellation
Or a few miserable boils!

But thou! Thou dost not turn thy face
Either to buffet or explore.
The devils bask, the martyrs weep.
Art thou too proud in a high place,
Or too befuddled in thy sleep?
Art thou too languorous to roar?

XII

You that we raised
To the high places,
With painted eyes
And cloudy faces,
You that are named,
But no one finds,
Made out of nothing
By men's minds—
Be true to us,
Play us not false;
Be cruel, O Gods,
Not fabulous.

You were our statues
Cut from space,
Gorgon's eyes
And dragon's face;
Fail us not,
You that we made,
When the stars go out
And the suns fade.
You were our hope
Death to bless—
Leave us not crying
In emptiness.

CRUSTACEAN REJOINDER

Take your great light away, your music end;
I'm off to feed myself as quick as I can.
You're perfectly impossible to comprehend,
I'm such a busy man.

Good God, haven't you got a circumference?
There's not a moment I can call my own—
My clocks, my keys, my wheels and instruments
And that fierce Ethiop, the telephone.

No doubt, it's very charming out in the sun,
But there are other things, you know. In any case,
I've got no time, no time. There's much to be done.
Thank God for this, my faithful carapace!

OUT OF TIME

I

I saw Time flowing like the hundred yachts
That fly behind the daylight, foxed with air;
Or piercing, like the quince-bright, bitter slats
Of sun gone thrusting under Harbour's hair.

So Time, the wave, enfolds me in its bed,
Or Time, the bony knife, it runs me through.
"Skulker, take heart," I thought my own heart said.
"The flood, the blade, go by—Time flows, not you!"

Vilely, continuously, stupidly,
Time takes me, drills me, drives through bone and vein,
So water bends the seaweeds in the sea,
The tide goes over, but the weeds remain.

Time, you must cry farewell, take up the track,
And leave this lovely moment at your back!

II

Time leaves the lovely moment at his back,
Eager to quench and ripen, kiss or kill;
To-morrow begs him, breathless for his lack,
Or beauty dead entreats him to be still.

His fate pursues him; he must open doors,
Or close them, for that pale and faceless host
Without a flag, whose agony implores
Birth, to be flesh, or funeral, to be ghost.

Out of all reckoning, out of dark and light,
Over the edges of dead Nows and Heres,
Blindly and softly, as a mistress might,
He keeps appointments with a million years.

I and the moment laugh, and let him go,
Leaning against his golden undertow.

III

Leaning against the golden undertow,
Backward, I saw the birds begin to climb
With bodies hailstone-clear, and shadows flow,
Fixed in a sweet meniscus, out of Time,

Out of the torrent, like the fainter land
Lensed in a bubble's ghostly camera,
The lighted beach, the sharp and china sand,
Glitters and waters and peninsula—

The moment's world, it was; and I was part,
Fleshless and ageless, changeless and made free.
"Fool, would you leave this country?" cried my heart,
But I was taken by the suck of sea.

The gulls go down, the body dies and rots,
And Time flows past them like a hundred yachts.

SLEEP

Do you give yourself to me utterly,
   Body and no-body, flesh and no-flesh,
Not as a fugitive, blindly or bitterly,
   But as a child might, with no other wish?
Yes, utterly.

Then I shall bear you down my estuary,
Carry you and ferry you to burial mysteriously,
Take you and receive you,
Consume you, engulf you,
In the huge cave, my belly, lave you
With huger waves continually.

And you shall cling and clamber there
And slumber there, in that dumb chamber,
Beat with my blood's beat, hear my heart move
Blindly in bones that ride above you,
Delve in my flesh, dissolved and bedded,
Through viewless valves embodied so—

Till daylight, the expulsion and awakening,
   The riving and the driving forth,
Life with remorseless forceps beckoning—
   Pangs and betrayal of harsh birth.

SENSUALITY

FEELING hunger and cold, feeling
Food, feeling fire, feeling
Pity and pain, tasting
Time in a kiss, tasting
Anger and tears, touching
Eyelids with lips, touching
Plague, touching flesh, knowing
Blood in the mouth, knowing
Laughter like flame, holding
Pickaxe and pen, holding
Death in the hand, hearing
Boilers and bells, hearing
Birds, hearing hail, smelling
Cedar and sweat, smelling
Petrol and sea, feeling
Hunger and cold, feeling
Food, feeling fire. . . .

Feeling.

LESBIA'S DAUGHTER

Lesbia's daughter, I shall tell no lie,
Here's no fit amber for such a dainty fly.
Let them embalm your beauty whoso can
In boastful odes, I'm a more honest man.

Lovers' abodes with poets' words are paved,
But prudent girls would get those vows engraved,
For brass than paper being something stronger
May last, it's more than like, a fortnight longer.

Where's the fine music that the fossil men
Of lost Lemuria brandished on a pen?
All tossed in earth—men, music, lovers gone—
And where's the lust a skull has for a bone?

If joy can turn a moment to a year,
Why take to Then and There what's meant for Here,
Or nurture for a cemetery tense
The curious pleasures of impermanence?

Look for no lovers on that later scene,
Let it avail you Are, who shall have Been,
Burnt utterly the stick you had to burn,
Lived once, loved well, gave thanks, and won't return.

THE KNIFE

The plough that marks on Harley's field
    In flying earth its print
Throws up, like death itself concealed,
    A fang of rosy flint,

A flake of stone, by fingers hewed
    Whose buried bones are gone,
All gone, with fingers, hunters, food,
    But still the knife lives on.

And well I know, when bones are nought,
    The blade of stone survives—
I, too, from clods of aching thought,
    Have turned up sharper knives.

COCK-CROW

THE cock's far cry
From lonely yards
Burdens the night
With boastful birds
That mop their wings
To make response—
A mess of songs
And broken sense.

So, when I slept,
I heard your call
(If lips long dead
Could answer still)
And snapped-off thoughts
Broke into clamour,
Like the night's throats
Heard by a dreamer.

NORTH COUNTRY

North Country, filled with gesturing wood,
With trees that fence, like archers' volleys,
The flanks of hidden valleys
Where nothing's left to hide

But verticals and perpendiculars,
Like rain gone wooden, fixed in falling,
Or fingers blindly feeling
For what nobody cares;

Or trunks of pewter, bangled by greedy death,
Stuck with black staghorns, quietly sucking,
And trees whose boughs go seeking,
And trees like broken teeth

With smoky antlers broken in the sky;
Or trunks that lie grotesquely rigid,
Like bodies blank and wretched
After a fool's battue,

As if they've secret ways of dying here
And secret places for their anguish
When boughs at last relinquish
Their clench of blowing air—

But this gaunt country, filled with mills and saws,
With butter-works and railway-stations
And public institutions,
And scornful rumps of cows,

North Country, filled with gesturing wood—
Timber's the end it gives to branches,
Cut off in cubic inches,
Dripping red with blood.

SOUTH COUNTRY

After the whey-faced anonymity
Of river-gums and scribbly-gums and bush,
After the rubbing and the hit of brush,
You come to the South Country

As if the argument of trees were done,
The doubts and quarrelling, the plots and pains,
All ended by these clear and gliding planes
Like an abrupt solution.

And over the flat earth of empty farms
The monstrous continent of air floats back
Coloured with rotting sunlight and the black,
Bruised flesh of thunderstorms:

Air arched, enormous, pounding the bony ridge,
Ditches and hutches, with a drench of light,
So huge, from such infinities of height,
You walk on the sky's beach

While even the dwindled hills are small and bare,
As if, rebellious, buried, pitiful,
Something below pushed up a knob of skull,
Feeling its way to air.

LAST TRAMS

I

THAT street washed with violet
Writes like a tablet
Of living here; that pavement
Is the metal embodiment
Of living here; those terraces
Filled with dumb presences
Lobbed over mattresses,
Lusts and repentances,
Ardours and solaces,
Passions and hatreds
And love in brass bedsteads...
Lost now in emptiness
Deep now in darkness
Nothing but nakedness,
Rails like a ribbon
And sickness of carbon
Dying in distances.

II

THEN, from the skeletons of trams,
Gazing at lighted rooms, you'll find
The black and Röntgen diagrams
Of window-plants across the blind

That print their knuckleduster sticks,
Their buds of gum, against the light
Like negatives of candlesticks
Whose wicks are lit by fluorite;

And shapes look out, or bodies pass,
Between the darkness and the flare,
Between the curtain and the glass,
Of men and women moving there.

So through the moment's needle-eye,
Like phantoms in the window-chink,
Their faces brush you as they fly,
Fixed in the shutters of a blink;

But whose they are, intent on what,
Who knows? They rattle into void,
Stars of a film without a plot,
Snippings of idiot celluloid.

ADVICE TO PSYCHOLOGISTS

You spies that pierce the mind with trenches,
   Feasting your eyes through private panes,
Who, not content with Heavenly stenches,
   Insist on taking up the drains,

For you I've only two suggestions,
   Who prowl with torches in this Bog—
Small good you'll get from asking questions;
   Walk on your nostrils, like a dog.

VESPER-SONG OF
THE REVEREND SAMUEL MARSDEN

My cure of souls, my cage of brutes,
Go lick and learn at these my boots!
When tainted highways tear a hole,
I bid my cobbler welt the sole.
O, ye that wear the boots of Hell,
Shall I not welt a soul as well?
    O, souls that leak with holes of sin,
    Shall I not let God's leather in,
    Or hit with sacramental knout
    Your twice-convicted vileness out?

Lord, I have sung with ceaseless lips
A tinker's litany of whips,
Have graved another Testament
On backs bowed down and bodies bent.
My stripes of jewelled blood repeat
A scarlet Grace for holy meat.
    Not mine, the Hand that writes the weal
    On this, my vellum of puffed veal,
    Not mine, the glory that endures,
    But Yours, dear God, entirely Yours.

Are there not Saints in holier skies
Who have been scourged to Paradise?
O, Lord, when I have come to that,
Grant there may be a Heavenly Cat
With twice as many tails as here—
    And make me, God, Your Overseer.
    But if the veins of Saints be dead,
    Grant me a whip in Hell instead,
    Where blood is not so hard to fetch.

But I, Lord, am Your humble wretch.

TO A FRIEND

Adam, because on the mind's roads
    Your mouth is always in a hurry,
Because you know 500 odes
    And 19 ways to make a curry,

Because you fall in love with words
    And whistle beauty forth to kiss them,
And blow the tails from China birds
    Whilst I continually miss them,

Because you top my angry best
    At billiards, fugues or pulling corks out,
And whisk a fritter from its nest
    Before there's time to hand the forks out,

Because you saw the Romans wink,
    Because your senses dance to metre,
Because, no matter what I drink,
    You'll hold at least another litre,

Because you've got a gipsy's eye
    That melts the rage of catamountains,
And metaphors that pass me by
    Burst from your lips in lovely fountains,

Because you've bitten the harsh foods
    Of life, grabbed every dish that passes,
And walked amongst the multitudes
    Without the curse of looking-glasses,

Because I burn the selfsame flame
    No falls of dirty earth may smother,
Oh, in your Abbey of Thélème,
    Enlist me as a serving-brother!

WILLIAM STREET

The red globes of light, the liquor-green,
The pulsing arrows and the running fire
Spilt on the stones, go deeper than a stream;
You find this ugly, I find it lovely.

Ghosts' trousers, like the dangle of hung men,
In pawnshop-windows, bumping knee by knee,
But none inside to suffer or condemn;
You find this ugly, I find it lovely.

Smells rich and rasping, smoke and fat and fish
And puffs of paraffin that crimp the nose,
Or grease that blesses onions with a hiss;
You find it ugly, I find it lovely.

The dips and molls, with flip and shiny gaze
(Death at their elbows, hunger at their heels)
Ranging the pavements of their pasturage;
You find it ugly, I find it lovely.

CANNIBAL STREET

"Buy, who'll buy," the pedlar sings,
"Bones of beggars, loins of kings,
Ribs of murder, haunch of hate,
And Beauty's head on a butcher's plate!"

Hook by hook, on steaming stalls,
The hero hangs, the harlot sprawls;
For Helen's flesh, in such a street,
Is only a kind of dearer meat.

"Buy, who'll buy," the pedlar begs,
"Angel-wings and lady-legs,
Tender bits and dainty parts—
Buy, who'll buy my skewered hearts?"

Buy, who'll buy? The cleavers fall,
The dead men creak, the live men call,
And I (God save me) bargained there,
Paid my pennies and ate my share.

TO THE POETRY* OF HUGH McCRAE

Uncles who burst on childhood, from the East,
Blown from air, like bearded ghosts arriving,
And are, indeed, a kind of guessed-at ghost
Through mumbled names at dinner-tables moving,

Bearers of parrots, bonfires of blazing stones,
Their pockets fat with riches out of reason,
Meerschaum and sharks'-teeth, ropes of China coins,
And weeds and seeds and berries blowzed with poison—

So, from the baleful Kimberleys of thought,
From the mad continent of dreams, you wander,
Spending your trophies at our bloodless feet,
Mocking our fortunes with more desperate plunder;

So with your boomerangs of rhyme you come,
With blossoms wrenched from sweet and deadly branches,
And we, pale Crusoes in the moment's tomb,
Watch, turn aside, and touch again those riches,

Nor ask what beaches of the mind you trod,
What skies endured, and unimagined rivers,
Or whiteness trenched by what mysterious tide,
And aching silence of the Never-Nevers;

Watch, turn aside, and touch with easy faith
Your chest of miracles, but counting nothing,
Or dumbly, that you stole them out of death,
Out of death's pyramids, to prove us breathing.

* *Poetry: An art practised by the ancients.*

We breathe, who beat the sides of emptiness,
We live, who die by statute in steel hearses,
We dance, whose only posture gives us grace
To squeeze the greasy udders of our purses—

(Look in this harsher glass, and I will show you
The daylight after the darkness, and the morning
After the midnight, and after the night the day
After the year after, terribly returning).

We live by these, your masks and images,
We breathe in this, your quick and borrowed body;
But you take passage on the ruffian seas,
And you are vanished in the dark already.

FULL ORCHESTRA

My words are the poor footmen of your pride,
Of what you cry, you trumpets, each to each
With mouths of air; my speech is the dog-speech
Of yours, the Roman tongue—but mine is tied
By harsher bridles, dumb with breath and bone.
Vainly it mocks the dingo strings, the stops,
The pear-tree flying in the flute, with drops
Of music, quenched and scattered by your own.

So serving-men, who run all night with wine,
And whet their ears, and crouch upon the floor,
Sigh broken words no man has heard before
Or since, but ravished in the candleshine,
Between the push and shutting of a door,
From the great table where their masters dine.

FIVE BELLS

*Time that is moved by little fidget wheels
Is not my Time, the flood that does not flow.
Between the double and the single bell
Of a ship's hour, between a round of bells
From the dark warship riding there below,
I have lived many lives, and this one life
Of Joe, long dead, who lives between five bells.*

Deep and dissolving verticals of light
Ferry the falls of moonshine down. Five bells
Coldly rung out in a machine's voice. Night and water
Pour to one rip of darkness, the Harbour floats
In air, the Cross hangs upside-down in water.

Why do I think of you, dead man, why thieve
These profitless lodgings from the flukes of thought
Anchored in Time? You have gone from earth,
Gone even from the meaning of a name;
Yet something's there, yet something forms its lips
And hits and cries against the ports of space,
Beating their sides to make its fury heard.

Are you shouting at me, dead man, squeezing your face
In agonies of speech on speechless panes?
Cry louder, beat the windows, bawl your name!

But I hear nothing, nothing... only bells,
Five bells, the bumpkin calculus of Time.
Your echoes die, your voice is dowsed by Life,
There's not a mouth can fly the pygmy strait—
Nothing except the memory of some bones
Long shoved away, and sucked away, in mud;

And unimportant things you might have done,
Or once I thought you did; but you forgot,
And all have now forgotten—looks and words
And slops of beer; your coat with buttons off,
Your gaunt chin and pricked eye, and raging tales
Of Irish kings and English perfidy,
And dirtier perfidy of publicans
Groaning to God from Darlinghurst.

Five bells.

Then I saw the road, I heard the thunder
Tumble, and felt the talons of the rain
The night we came to Moorebank in slab-dark,
So dark you bore no body, had no face,
But a sheer voice that rattled out of air
(As now you'd cry if I could break the glass),
A voice that spoke beside me in the bush,
Loud for a breath or bitten off by wind,
Of Milton, melons, and the Rights of Man,
And blowing flutes, and how Tahitian girls
Are brown and angry-tongued, and Sydney girls
Are white and angry-tongued, or so you'd found.
But all I heard was words that didn't join
So Milton became melons, melons girls,
And fifty mouths, it seemed, were out that night,
And in each tree an Ear was bending down,
Or something had just run, gone behind grass,
When, blank and bone-white, like a maniac's thought,
The naphtha-flash of lightning slit the sky,
Knifing the dark with deathly photographs.
There's not so many with so poor a purse
Or fierce a need, must fare by night like that,
Five miles in darkness on a country track,
But when you do, that's what you think.

Five bells.

In Melbourne, your appetite had gone,
Your angers too; they had been leeched away
By the soft archery of summer rains
And the sponge-paws of wetness, the slow damp
That stuck the leaves of living, snailed the mind,
And showed your bones, that had been sharp with rage,
The sodden ecstasies of rectitude.
I thought of what you'd written in faint ink,
Your journal with the sawn-off lock, that stayed behind
With other things you left, all without use,
All without meaning now, except a sign
That someone had been living who now was dead:
"At Labassa. Room 6 x 8
On top of the tower; because of this, very dark
And cold in winter. Everything has been stowed
Into this room—500 books all shapes
And colours, dealt across the floor
And over sills and on the laps of chairs;
Guns, photoes of many differant things
And differant curioes that I obtained...."

In Sydney, by the spent aquarium-flare
Of penny gaslight on pink wallpaper,
We argued about blowing up the world,
But you were living backward, so each night
You crept a moment closer to the breast,
And they were living, all of them, those frames
And shapes of flesh that had perplexed your youth,
And most your father, the old man gone blind,
With fingers always round a fiddle's neck,
That graveyard mason whose fair monuments
And tablets cut with dreams of piety
Rest on the bosoms of a thousand men
Staked bone by bone, in quiet astonishment
At cargoes they had never thought to bear,
These funeral-cakes of sweet and sculptured stone.

Where have you gone? The tide is over you,
The turn of midnight water's over you,
As Time is over you, and mystery,
And memory, the flood that does not flow.
You have no suburb, like those easier dead
In private berths of dissolution laid—
The tide goes over, the waves ride over you
And let their shadows down like shining hair,
But they are Water; and the sea-pinks bend
Like lilies in your teeth, but they are Weed;
And you are only part of an Idea.
I felt the wet push its black thumb-balls in,
The night you died, I felt your eardrums crack,
And the short agony, the longer dream,
The Nothing that was neither long nor short;
But I was bound, and could not go that way,
But I was blind, and could not feel your hand.
If I could find an answer, could only find
Your meaning, or could say why you were here
Who now are gone, what purpose gave you breath
Or seized it back, might I not hear your voice?

I looked out of my window in the dark
At waves with diamond quills and combs of light
That arched their mackerel-backs and smacked the sand
In the moon's drench, that straight enormous glaze,
And ships far off asleep, and Harbour-buoys
Tossing their fireballs wearily each to each,
And tried to hear your voice, but all I heard
Was a boat's whistle, and the scraping squeal
Of seabirds' voices far away, and bells,
Five bells. Five bells coldly ringing out.
                                         Five bells.

POLARITIES

Sometimes she is like sherry, like the sun through a vessel of glass,
Like light through an oriel window in a room of yellow wood;
Sometimes she is the colour of lions, of sand in the fire of noon,
Sometimes as bruised with shadows as the afternoon.

Sometimes she moves like rivers, sometimes like trees;
Or tranced and fixed like South Pole silences;
Sometimes she is beauty, sometimes fury, sometimes neither,
Sometimes nothing, drained of meaning, null as water.

Sometimes, when she makes pea-soup or plays me Schumann,
I love her one way; sometimes I love her another
More disturbing way when she opens her mouth in the dark;
Sometimes I like her with camellias, sometimes with a parsley-stalk,
Sometimes I like her swimming in a mirror on the wall;
Sometimes I don't like her at all.

AN INSCRIPTION FOR DOG RIVER*

Our general was the greatest and bravest of generals.
For his deeds, look around you on this coast—
Here is his name cut next to Ashur-Bani-Pal's,
Nebuchadnezzar's and the Roman host;
And we, though our identities have been lost,
Lacking the validity of stone or metal,
We, too, are part of his memorial,
Having been put in for the cost,

Having bestowed on him all we had to give
In battles few can recollect,
Our strength, obedience and endurance,
Our wits, our bodies, our existence,
Even our descendants' right to live—
Having given him everything, in fact,
Except respect.

---

* "At this point the hills approach the sea and rise high above the river; together they form a very serious obstacle which had to be negotiated by every army marching along the shore. Here the Egyptian Pharaohs therefore commemorated their successes, and their example was followed by all subsequent conquerors, Assyrian, Babylonian, Roman (and French) down to 1920."—*Steimatzky's Guide to Syria and the Lebanon.* In 1942, General Sir Thomas Blamey had an inscription cut to celebrate the capture of Damour by Australian troops under his command.

BEACH BURIAL

Softly and humbly to the Gulf of Arabs
The convoys of dead sailors come;
At night they sway and wander in the waters far under,
But morning rolls them in the foam.

Between the sob and clubbing of the gunfire
Someone, it seems, has time for this,
To pluck them from the shallows and bury them in burrows
And tread the sand upon their nakedness;

And each cross, the driven stake of tidewood,
Bears the last signature of men,
Written with such perplexity, with such bewildered pity,
The words choke as they begin—

"*Unknown seaman*"—the ghostly pencil
Wavers and fades, the purple drips,
The breath of the wet season has washed their inscriptions
As blue as drowned men's lips,

Dead seamen, gone in search of the same landfall,
Whether as enemies they fought,
Or fought with us, or neither; the sand joins them together,
Enlisted on the other front.

El Alamein.

SOME NOTES ON THE POEMS

1. "FIVE VISIONS OF CAPTAIN COOK"*

In discussing my own poems, I shall try to answer some of the questions most frequently asked by the students whose fate it is to have to wrestle with them—a situation I would have foreseen with horror in the days when I toiled at school myself, cursing the authors of the set pieces. It may be taken as a sign of increased tolerance, as well as of the lively interest in Australian writing now kindled in the schools, that I receive several hundred letters of inquiry from school students every year, all couched in the politest and even kindliest terms.

It is difficult for any writer to discuss his own verse, mainly because of the problem of deciding where the boundary lies between the personal associations and meanings which certain words produce in him and those which they produce in the reader. In any case, the very act of analysing emotional documents composed twenty or thirty years ago is often impossible for the author—he may feel that he is in the position of a palaeontologist asked to report on a specimen of fossilized fern.

The sequence of poems called "Five Visions of Captain Cook" is, I think, quite straightforward in its intention and expression. It could be described as a sort of Identikit likeness, made by superimposing a number of aspects of Cook, seen through the eyes of various men who sailed with him, thus approaching perhaps a total portrait.

The first vision of Cook is that of the ordinary seaman who manned his ships on the three great voyages. The second is that of some of the officers who served under him.

---

* From a lecture given at the University of N.S.W., 1965, reprinted in *Bread and Wine*, Sydney, Angus and Robertson, 1970.

The third is the view of history (denoted by the time-measuring instruments in Cook's cabin). The fourth is that of some of the midshipmen. The fifth is the vision of Cook which remained in the memory of one of his companions many years after his death.

The whole work owes a great debt to a remarkable man whom I was once privileged to know and visit, Captain Francis Bayldon, who lived at Darling Point in the '20s and who died in 1948. Captain Bayldon was a sea-captain himself, if not of the "powder days" at least of the clipper ship days of last century. From sail he transferred to steam in 1901 and commanded many Burns Philp vessels in the Pacific until 1910, charting previously unsurveyed anchorages for the Hydrographic Office. In 1910 he founded the Sydney Nautical School (in which hundreds of Australian merchant service officers have been trained). He was an authority on the history of Pacific navigation, especially on Torres and Cook, and his reconstruction of Cook's *Endeavour* was published as a plate. But above all he had a magnificent nautical library, more than a thousand books about the sea and seamen, logs, journals, learned papers, instruction manuals, maps and charts, many of them exceedingly rare and valuable. Fortunately the Mitchell Library acquired them after his death.

Since he was my wife's uncle, I was allowed to browse through this collection on my weekly visits. Over a glass of sherry I was encouraged to ask questions, and his enthusiasm, his scholarly gusto and his astonishing knowledge of unfamiliar details soon infected me with his own worship of Cook. Indeed, all that I have written about Captain Cook I got from Captain Bayldon. The *Five Visions*, rough and incomplete as they seem to me still, are merely fragments of the image he built for me.

In *part 1*, there are two principal themes—the contrast between the old kind of sea captain and the modern kind, and the crucial decision which brought Cook to the coast of Australia.

The ship's captain of the days of sail and "powder" (gunpowder) was required to have some working knowledge of such things as mathematics, astronomy, navigation, chart-reading, sight-taking, foreign languages and elementary medicine, attainments which made him seem an almost supernatural being in the eyes of his crew, most of whom were unable to read or write. The simple sailors under his command did what they were bidden, sailed where they were taken, ate and drank what they were given, blindly confident that the magic of their captain (as it must have seemed to them) would preserve their lives from evil spirits, monsters and spells (some of them still believed in sea-serpents) and convey them safely across unmapped seas and unknown lands.

Captains like this were indeed "daemons in wigs", navigating by signs in the stars which they could read as easily as books, though to ordinary men the sky seemed just a tangle of constellations. They gave their crews medicaments and drugs against disease (in Cook's case against scurvy), which seemed nonsense to the sailors but which they swallowed with childish faith. The success of such commanders depended above all on their personal qualities, their individual resources of courage, nerve, imagination, shrewdness and self-confidence.

"*No laws of schoolbook steam*" expresses this idea. The speed of a passage by sail (and in consequence its profitability to the owners of the ship) were often determined by the captain's daring and skill in such things as putting on full sail in a high wind and knowing when it could be done and at what risk. In modern days of steam and oil, the captain is limited by the purely mechanical factor of the ship's engines and their capacities. The boiler-plates will take just so much pressure before blowing up. There is no call, therefore, for the same kind of personal nerve or judgement in deciding what sails to use or risks to run. The modern skipper is often an "executive of company rules", bound not to take any undue chances.

Thus we have two aspects of the old sailing-ship captain. (1) In the eyes of his crew, a magically gifted being whose orders (daft as they might seem) could save their lives. (2) A man on whose personal characteristics of audacity and self-confidence the success of the enterprise often depended. This was the kind of captain Cook was, and the first section of *part 1* draws a distinction between the "powder days" and the modern reign of "company rules".

In the second section, we have Cook coming to the Coral Sea, at the north of the Australian coastline, after his voyage to New Zealand. This was the great turning-point for earlier explorers who depended on sails. If they went west, they turned against the prevailing winds, with no indication of how long their provisions would need to last, or what lay in store for them, or whether indeed they would ever come back. It was in every respect a "passage into the dark". But if they turned north, into Torres Strait, the winds would be with them all their way home through the Indian Ocean.

It was a fateful decision to have to make, and most of those who confronted it—including Tasman and Bougainville—had chosen the path of prudence by sailing north. Bougainville recorded that he had heard "the voice of God" advising him to take the safe way home to the north, away from the "dead lee shore". But Captain Cook, at these crossroads of navigation and history, determined to sail west instead of north, "into the devil's mouth", and so came to the coastline of eastern Australia—and so, 160 years later, I was able to write this poem.

The historical facts to which *part 2* alludes are verified by the journals, logs, diaries and letters of Cook and many of the people who accompanied him.

"*Cook sailed at night.*" Usually, in strange waters, particularly in such an area of hidden reefs and unsounded depths, sailing was done in daylight only. But such was Cook's confidence in his navigation and seamanship that he kept his vessel sailing in darkness as well. No doubt he felt that he had only a limited time for exploration and did not wish to waste a minute.

The episode in which the ship narrowly missed hitting a coral reef while officers stood on deck taking their sights for longitude has been described by Captain Cook himself. The greatest danger of sailing in such waters was the risk of a current driving a ship on to a sharp reef with no wind to take it off. The Australian sailor-writer Alan Villiers has written of this incident: "The little ship drifted until she was only the trough of the sea away from a horrible reef over which the surf boiled and the great Coral Sea rollers smashed in fury. A few yards more and not a soul aboard nor an undamaged plank of the ship would have survived."

This is what Cook wrote: "The same sea that washed the side of the ship rose in a breaker prodigiously high the very next time it did arise, so that between us and destruction was only a dismal valley, the breadth of one wave, and even now no ground could be felt with 120 fathoms. Messrs Green, Clerke and Forwood were engaged in taking a sight for the longitude."

Alan Villiers remarked: "For three of the most important officers in the ship calmly to proceed with the accumulation of precise data to work out laboriously some reasonable approximation of the longitude of the ship, when that same ship was five minutes from one of the nastiest pieces of reef in the Coral Sea, and when the great swell was edging them to their deaths—this is on a level with the great moments of the sea. Messrs Green, Clerke and Forwood were perfectly aware of the danger the ship was in because, before they had the data for their sights, the foam from the reef was making a fine spray on their instruments."

In *part 3*, the allusion is to an aspect of the second voyage which would have made it memorable in history even if nothing else had been achieved. This time Cook took with him two recently invented chronometers, installed by the Admiralty for a trial of the new method of discovering longitude. Thus he was, in effect, a test-pilot trying out new equipment.

In the episode described in *part 2*, the officers used the "lunar" method, involving complicated calculations, which was only a little less unsatisfactory than the even older method of the log line. Sir Isaac Newton suggested a new way, by the comparison of two clocks, one marked Greenwich time and the other the local time by the sun at sea. The great problem was to construct a clock which would keep absolutely accurate time through the vast range of temperature and humidity of a sea-voyage.

Two famous English watchmakers supplied the chronometers for this historic experiment. One was made by John Arnold, a friend of Sir Joseph Banks, the other by Larcum Kendal from a prototype invented by John Harrison. After both had been tested for many months of Cook's voyage, it was found that Kendal's chronometer lost time (7 minutes, 45 seconds in three years) while Arnold's gained time. For the purpose of the poem, it is imagined therefore that Kendal lived in the past and Arnold in the future.

In *part 4*, the vision of Captain Cook on a workaday occasion during his third voyage is derived from some verses written by one of the midshipmen aboard, later to become Captain Trevenen. I was able to see a copy of this manuscript among the treasures of Captain Bayldon's library. The phrase "cats to catch mice" was one of Cook's favourite admonitions to the lively boys who were his midshipmen. It is quoted by Trevenen with the explanation that the captain frequently told them that he didn't mind how much they kicked up their heels provided they did their duties first—his actual words were "my cats have to catch mice before they get any milk".

So, after their routines had been finished, these young schoolboy-officers, to whom the whole voyage with all its perils and hardships was a glorious adventure, were often able to go with Cook in one of the ship's boats when he made small excursions, noting details for his charts and getting fresh meat for the galley from birds and animals ashore.

The account of Cook in *part 5* comes in substance from the manuscript journal kept by Captain Alexander Home. I had the fortune to see a copy of it in Captain Bayldon's library. Like Captain Trevenen, Alexander Home had been one of Cook's company on his third voyage. Later, after many years at sea, he became almost totally blind and retired on a pension of 2s. 6d. a day to his home in Berwickshire in Scotland. Although Captain Home did not witness the affray in which Cook lost his life, he wrote a narrative of it soon after the event, from statements made by those who had been ashore at the time. The references to Cook (such as his warning to deserters that he would get them back eventually "dead or alive") are almost word for word from Home's journal.

The line "*Greenwich Hospital for Cook*" alludes to the Admiralty's offer to give Cook an administrative post at the home for naval veterans, Greenwich Hospital. This was at a time when his proposals for further voyages were becoming a nuisance to the lethargic sea lords. For Cook, then aged 47, it was a dreadful vision of stagnation and he was reluctant to accept the offer. It would, indeed, have been like putting a seagull in a birdcage.

The details of the killing of Captain Cook follow the accepted version given in many descriptions of the scene. It is a fact that Cook was stabbed with an English knife that had been traded to the Hawaiian natives only a few days before.

2. "FIVE BELLS" AND OTHER POEMS*

Many hundreds of years ago, in an Arabian fairytale, a man dipped his head into a basin of magic water. In the

* First published in the *Daily Telegraph*, 31st July, 1967; reprinted in *Bread and Wine*, Sydney, Angus and Robertson, 1970.

few moments between submerging his face and withdrawing it, he dreamed that he had sailed on seven voyages, was cast up in a shipwreck, captured by pirates, discovered a diamond as big as a turkey's egg, married a princess, fought in many battles, and was brought to execution.

After he had lived this whole lifetime, he opened his eyes and shook the water from his face and found himself amongst a laughing group of people, with everything around him exactly as it had been when he had dipped his head into the water five seconds before.

I think the point of this story is that, although the man's lifetime under water had been a vision, the experiences which he suffered during it, the miseries and delights, the fears and triumphs, were as actual as those of his real life. He had, in fact, lived an entire existence on another time-scale.

This is partly the idea of "Five Bells", a poem which suggests that the whole span of a human life can be imagined, and even vicariously experienced, in a flash of thought as brief as the interval between the strokes of a bell. "Five Bells" can be described as a kind of meditation at night, while looking at Sydney Harbour and hearing the cold fact of time, five bells or half-past ten, rung from a ship at its moorings below.

But in the three seconds or so which this mechanical process involves, between the double ding-ding and the single ding of the ship's bell, a sequence from a very different time-scale is interposed, compressing about thirty years of human life into the three seconds. For this reason the words "*five bells*" are repeated three times during the poem, to remind the reader that time, on the other scale, has occupied only a few moments, that the tongue of the bell is still moving and the sound is still suspended in the air.

The poem therefore is on two planes. First it attempts to epitomize the life of a specific human being, but fundamentally it is an expression of the relativeness of "time".

Considered in this light, the personal allusions are unimportant. However, so many students continue to inquire about the identity of "Joe" and the circumstances of his death that a little explanation may be justified.

The "dead man" whose life is re-lived "between the double and the single bell" was named Joe Lynch. He was a friend of my youth, a black-and-white artist of superb humour and talent whose work appeared in the '20s in many Australian periodicals and who was a member of the staffs of *Smith's Weekly* and Melbourne *Punch* when I, too, worked for them. (He was a brother of the sculptor Frank, or "Guy", Lynch, whose "Satyr" and "Australian Venus" were famous in the '30s. Frank Lynch was old-fashioned enough to believe that sculpture should primarily be a work of beauty rather than of scrap iron and wire, and as a consequence his magnificent Satyr now moulders in the cellars of the Sydney Art Gallery.)

One evening in the 1930s, Joe and half a dozen other artists and journalists left Circular Quay by ferry to go to a party of the north side of the Harbour. Joe sat on the lower deck-rail of the boat, clad in an ancient tattered raincoat, heavily laden with bottled beer in the pockets. There was a good deal of jollity until someone noticed that Joe had disappeared. The ferry hove to and there was a wide search, but no trace of Joe Lynch could be found. His body was never recovered and eventually he was presumed drowned.

There are a number of lines in "Five Bells" which seem to cause constant inquiries from students, and I shall try to explain some of them.

"*. . . the Cross hangs upside-down in water.*" This, of course, means the reflection of the Southern Cross constellation and is *not* (as one ingenious school-student suggested) an allusion to the lights of Kings Cross.

"*Your journal with the sawn-off lock . . .*" In his bedroom at a North Melbourne boarding-house in the days when he worked for *Punch*, Joe found a battered, morocco-bound notebook, apparently the relic of some unknown lodger, and gave it to me for scribbling. It contained some pages of manuscript notes written by the lodger (or Joe) which, of course, I had really no right to see.

One of these entries is reproduced literally in "Five Bells". Its misspellings ("photoes", "differant", "curioes") give it, I think, a peculiarly haunting and convincing flavour. I imagine that Labassa, at the beginning of the extract, is the name of another Melbourne lodging-house and that the writer is describing his bedroom "at the top of the tower". But for the purpose of the poem I have assumed that this is Joe's own entry.

"*We argued about blowing up the world.*" Joe was a devout nihilist and frequently contended (over a pint of Victoria bitter) that the only remedy for the world's disease was to blow it up and start afresh. He meant this literally and—long before the discovery of nuclear fission—conceived the notion of an explosive force that would destroy the entire globe at one go.

"*Harbour-buoys/Tossing their fireballs wearily each to each.*" No pun on "boys" is intended, as some critics have suggested, though there may have been a subconscious Empsonian instinct. It is an attempt to describe the Harbour navigation-lights, winking alternately on each side of the channel, so that it might appear that one was throwing a "fireball" to be caught by the other.

"Country Towns" is a small and simple Australian bucolic which requires (I hope) no elucidation. It refers to no country town specifically but is a composite of many which have seemed the same. Its period is fading, or perhaps has already vanished, since farmers today prefer motors to mares and buggy-wheels are seldom heard. However, it is possible that the last of the Hogans still manage a few supermarkets and that the playbills of the Great Golightly Family may still be found under a layer of posters advertising pop singers.

As a matter of accuracy, it might be mentioned that

"locusts" should properly be called cicadas and that the "pepper-trees" are those feathery small trees, with bunches of red pellets, more scientifically known as Peruvian mastic.

"North Country" and "South Country" are located in the coastal areas north and south of Sydney, and the contrast is between the densely timbered forests of the north and the bare, rolling cattle-grazing hills of the south. In "North Country", the phrase "bangled by greedy death" means "ringbarked". Seven lines further down, "battue" is intended to suggest that the dismembered trunks of felled trees resemble the bodies of animals slaughtered in a game-shooting hunt or "battue".

"William Street" is a sort of flashlight photograph of the swarming city channel that runs up the hill to Kings Cross, taken on a rainy night when the surface of the road is coated with a slick of reds and greens and whites reflected from the neon skysigns (the "red globes" and "pulsing arrows").

Here, too, there have been inexorable changes since the poem was written. The old fish-shops and "21 meals for £1" cafes have given way to pizza-counters and American hamburger-bars, and second-hand clothes no longer hang in pawnshop windows. But the general reason for the poem remains, since it was intended as a defence of metropolitan fascinations against those who considered the city "ugly" and found beauty only in the outback.

"Sleep" is explained by its title. It imagines the nightly human mystery of going to sleep as a surrender to complete selflessness, in the form of a return to the unconsciousness of a child in its mother's body. Thus the nature of sleeping is pictured as the oblivion of pre-life and that of awakening as birth itself.

Sleep, the state of unconsciousness, is personified as the mother addressing the child, the sleeper. The response "*Yes, utterly,*" comes from the sleeper—or child—consenting to the total immersion of "body and no-body, flesh and no-flesh" (that is to say, body and mind) within the enveloping ocean of unconsciousness.

Technically this poem is an experiment in the narcotic effect of the repetition of certain consonant-structures and vowel-sounds. The significant vowel-sound is the long "U" in such words and phrases as "bear you", "estuary", "carry you", "ferry you", "take you", "receive you", "consume you", "engulf you", "huge cave" and "huger waves". There are also many internal rhymes and assonances such as "ferry" and "burial", "cave", "lave", "waves", "slumber", "dumb", "remorseless", "forceps", and so on.

"Beach Burial" comes from the period when Australian soldiers were fighting in the Western Desert of Egypt near El Alamein, where the German advance had been halted in 1942. Many of their camps were on the Mediterranean coast, and in the morning it was not uncommon to find the bodies of drowned men washed up on the beaches. They were buried in the sandhills under improvised crosses, identification usually being impossible. Most of them were sailors, some British, some German or Italian, some of them "neutrals".

Many of the inquiries from students about this poem have asked the meaning of its last words *"other front"*. The superficial meaning, of course, is a military one. The verses were written at a time when there was pressure on the Allies to open a "second front" against the Germans.

However, there is a deeper implication which is really the theme of the poem. It is the idea that all men of all races, whether they fight with each other or not, are engaged together on the common "front" of humanity's existence. The absolute fact of death unites them. Their hatreds, quarrels and wars should be dwarfed by the huger human struggle to survive against disease and cataclysms on this dangerous planet.

KENNETH SLESSOR

INDEX TO FIRST LINES

INDEX TO FIRST LINES

A bird sang in the jaws of night	100
A ship in hell marooned	42
Adam, because on the mind's roads	116
After all, you are my rather tedious hero	64
After the candles had gone out, and those	71
After the whey-faced anonymity	112
And who are we to argue with our lutes	96
At five I wake, rise, rub on the smoking pane	17
"Bees of old Spanish wine	34
Burying friends is not a pomp	81
But Life we know, but Life we know	101
But who are we to sneer	95
"Buy, who'll buy," the pedlar sings	118
Camazotz and Anubis	97
Captain Dobbin, having retired from the South Seas	51
Chafing on flags of ebony and pearl	10
Come in your painted coaches, friends of mine	49
Coming out of India with ten thousand a year	90
Cook was a captain of the Admiralty	67
Country towns, with your willows and squares	84
Do you give yourself to me utterly	106
Earth which has known so many passages	88
Feeling hunger and cold, feeling	107
Flowers turned to stone! Not all the botany	68

Gas flaring on the yellow platform; voices running up and down	39
Good roaring pistol-boys, brave lads of gold	32
Gutted of station, noise alone	82
Here in a gulf of golden leaf	62
I saw Time flowing like the hundred yachts	104
If all those tumbling babes of heaven	7
I'll kick your walls to bits, I'll die scratching a tunnel	86
In an old play-house, in an old play	94
In and out the countryfolk, the carriages and carnival	44
In the apple-country, in the apple-trees	46
In the castle of Glubbdubdrib	77
In the old play-house, in the watery flare	94
In the pans of straw-coned country	44
In Undine's mirror the cutpurse found	35
Jackey Jackey gallops on a horse like a swallow	85
Late: a cold smear of sunlight bathes the room	13
Leaning against the golden undertow	105
Lesbia's daughter, I shall tell no lie	108
Look up! Thou hast a shining Guest	50
Marduk his jewelled finger flips	95
Music, on the air's edge, rides alone	42
My cure of souls, my cage of brutes	115
My strings I break, my breast I beat	101
My words are the poor footmen of your pride	120
Nay, 'tis no Devil's walk	19
No pause! The buried pipes ring out	36
No wind of Life may strike within	59

North Country, filled with gesturing wood	111
Nothing grows on the stone trees	48
Now the statues lean over each to each, and sing	40
O, silent night, dark beach	43
Once, at your words, I would have struck to flame	47
Once long ago lived a Flea	93
Once Mermaids mocked your ships	60
Open! It is the moon knocking with fists of air	46
Our general was the greatest and bravest of generals	126
Post-roads that clapped with tympan heels	58
Ranks of electroplated cubes, dwindling to glitters	87
Reading how Marco Polo came	8
Scaly with poison, bright with flame	4
Shall I give you the Bourbon-sugars	66
"Shang Ya! I want to be your friend"	98
Smoke upon smoke; over the stone lips	37
So quiet it was in that high, sun-steeped room	3
Softly and humbly to the Gulf of Arabs	127
Sometimes she is like sherry, like the sun through a vessel of glass	125
Sometimes the god would fold his wings	70
Sophie, in shocks of scarlet lace	75
Sophie's my world . . . my arm must soon or later	38
Suddenly to become John Benbow, walking down William Street	92
Take your great light away, your music end	103
"Talbingo River"—as one says of bones	83
Ten bottles of Calcavillo . . . one pot of Honey	25
That street washed with violet	113

The cock's far cry	110
The King of Cuckooz Contrey	56
The old orchard, full of smoking air	74
The old Quarry, Sun, with bleeding scales	39
The plough that marks on Harley's field	109
The red globes of light, the liquor-green	117
The smell of birds' nests faintly burning	65
Then, from the skeletons of trams	113
There were strange riders once, came gusting down	1
"These are the floating berries of the night	33
These black bush-waters, heavy with crusted boughs	11
Thief of the moon, thou robber of old delight	12
This is really a Complete Life and Works	99
This Water, like a sky that no one uses	76
Those friends of Lao-Tzu, those wise old men	6
Thou moon, like a white Christus hanging	82
Time leaves the lovely moment at his back	104
Time that is moved by little fidget wheels	121
Torches and running fire; the flagstones drip	45
Transports of field nerves; a wistful cough	91
Two chronometers the captain had	69
Uncles who burst on childhood, from the East	119
Venus with rosy-cloven rump	79
When to those Venusbergs, thy breasts	18
You spies that pierce the mind with trenches	114
You that we raised	102